A Light Shines in GOD'S Country

IRENE BURNS

A Strang Company

A Light Shines in God's Country by Irene Burns
Published by Creation House
A Strang Company
600 Rinehart Road
Lake Mary, Florida 32746
www.creationhouse.com

Unless otherwise noted, all Scripture quotations are from the King James Version of the Bible.

Scripture quotations marked NKJV are from the New King James Version of the Bible. Copyright © 1979, 1980, 1982 by Thomas Nelson, Inc., publishers. Used by permission.

Scripture quotations marked NIV are from the Holy Bible, New International Version of the Bible. Copyright © 1973, 1978, 1984, International Bible Society. Used by permission.

Cover design by Jerry Pomales

Library of Congress Control Number: 2007934642
International Standard Book Number: 978-1-59979-242-2

First Edition

08 09 10 11 12 — 987654321

Printed in the United States of America

Dedication

THIS BOOK IS gratefully and lovingly dedicated to Rev. Alton Shea. We all are eternally—literally—grateful to him for bringing us the wonderful message of Christ. To do this, it was necessary for him to diligently perform the herculean task of traveling over the hilly and often icy roads to the little college town to preach, then rush back more than ten miles to preach, and often sing, in his own church—on the radio—Sunday after Sunday.

Because of this great effort, he was brought into our lives. And because of his great effort, we all are now "safe in the arms of Jesus."

Precious Sir, may Jesus bless you beyond all you could ask or think. We love you and are so grateful—and will be for eternity!

Acknowledgments

THIS BOOK WOULD not exist if it had not been for the gracious diligence of our granddaughter, Alicia Pielow, who carefully deciphered my handwriting—no easy task! Thank you so much, Honey!

I also want to especially thank Mrs. Betty Burdick whose thoughtful kindness greatly helped to "open our ears and hearts" the the life-changing message of the gospel.

I am sincerely grateful and indebted to all who so kindly prayed for and helped us as we were living the book and to those who prayed that it would come to be a book. May the Lord bless each of you, and may all of you reap bountifully the kindnesses you have sown.

But above all, to God be the glory! Truly, great things He has done.

Contents

Foreword

THIS IS THE story of my family—my dear, exuberant, adventuresome, precious family—and the amazing, wonderful man that started it all. It will be hard to start slowly and build up into it, because of the joy I feel as I think of them. But bear with me, and I'll try not to make the beginning so tedious that you'll be asleep before the excitement starts.

But before we go on, I want to be sure to mention Don's amazing musical abilities. He took clarinet lessons for seven years, and played first clarinet in the high school band and orchestra. He then went on to teach himself saxophone, piano, guitar, and keyboard. He also plays bass guitar on our church worship team.

Don's enjoyment in playing is contagious and a real blessing with the Dixie Boys, and recently the Chariots, in various community festivals, nursing homes, churches, and, of course, our family events.

May the Lord bless each of you as you read. May He show you that He is "an ever-present help in trouble" (Psalm 46:1, NIV) and that children, far from being an annoyance and an irritation, are a reward from the Lord! (See Psalm 127:3.) (They sure do add spice to life!) A little P.S. to the reader: every single incident in this is absolutely true, and I have been very careful to avoid any exaggerations. Also, the names of all the "extras" have been changed.

1

Adventures Are Slow to Start

MY HUSBAND AND I met in high school at the end of our sophomore year. My father had been transferred up from Baltimore, Maryland, to Poughkeepsie, New York, with his company. My mom, two sisters, and I joined him by train after the house was sold and the movers had finished packing the truck.

I entered the co-ed high school coming from a sedate, all-girl, city public high school where one of the goals of the school was to mold young girls into young ladies—a goal which I sincerely hope the school still holds today. We were not allowed to use any slang words, nor have chewing gum on school grounds! And of course, without those wild creatures called boys around, things were a lot calmer; polished floors, large plants in the halls, with wooden benches nearby. In the lobby, under glass and on a marble podium, was a replica of the Declaration of Independence—something that meant a lot to me. In fact, I worked at copying its handwriting style. (Maybe that's why mine is a bit difficult to read!)

We had marvelous music in the assemblies. Each girl's voice was tested, and she was placed in the auditorium according to first soprano, second soprano, alto, and tenor. We sophomores sat up in the balcony, and the blend of more than one thousand voices wafting up to us was just beautiful.

One of the songs we sang was a rendition of Psalm 27:1, 3, 5:

> The Lord is my light,
> And my salvation.
> Whom, then, shall I fear?
> Whom, then, shall I fear?
> The Lord is the strength of my life.
> The Lord is the strength of my life.
> Of whom, then, shall I be afraid?
> Though a host should rise up against me.
> Yet shall my heart not be afraid.
> Though there rose up wars against me,
> Yet shall my heart not be afraid.
> For in the time of trouble
> He shall hide me in His tabernacle.
> Yea, in the secret places of His dwelling
> Shall He hide me,
> And set me up upon a rock of stone!
> The Lord is my life...

The school had a full orchestra with a magnificent set of copper kettledrums, and the singing, with the orchestral accompaniment, was truly wonderful.

We all stood to our feet when our principal, Miss Zouck, entered and walked up the aisle to greet us and begin the assembly. This gesture instilled in us a sense of respect, and I wonder what the impact would be on our culture if each school practiced just that gesture—standing when the school's head entered their assemblies.

Because of all this, I experienced a bit of culture shock in the new high school, especially seeing students in the halls chewing gum with open mouths! Believe me, being shy of nature, I didn't "look to the right or the left."

Just a little aside: when I was a child in Baltimore, each school day was begun with the reading of Scripture—usually a psalm. A different student read each day and then led the class in reciting the Lord's Prayer and the pledge to the American flag which was in the corner of each room. This was done through eighth grade. Our little fourth grade teacher's favorite Scripture passage was Psalm 46, and to please her, it was often chosen. To this day that Psalm is in my memory. And to be honest, when I would come into the classroom and see that inexpensive black Bible standing up on the teacher's desk with other books, it actually gave me a peaceful feeling, a feeling of security.

My grandparents gave me a similar Bible when I was about ten years old, and I began to read it. And my mother taught me to never put anything on top of a Bible. It is a book of honor.

The danger of identity theft has recently been in the news. It makes one wonder if, had we not forbidden the Scriptures as a part of our children's education forty-some years ago, things would be different. After all, "Thou shalt not steal" is part of the Ten Commandments.

But back to my entry into the scary co-ed high school world. There was a young redhead, also shy and also a sophomore, who was walking by the art room with a friend and noticed me. (Bless his heart, he says it was like, "Boing!") He had a friend, who was in my music theory class, introduce us.

This took place in the auditorium, and after I left, Don—the redhead—ran and took a flying leap off the stage, over the stairs and to the doorway, because, he says, he was so happy I had accepted a date for the movies with him.

Another friend happened to come into the auditorium when Don became airborne, and told the track coach, who sent someone to measure the distance. They were pretty surprised and immediately the coach drafted Don onto the team. It was a very different and quite exciting experience for me to watch him compete—especially since I had no brothers and had transferred from an all-girl high school. His specialty was the running broad jump—and his record of twenty feet, four inches stood for quite a few years. It would have been even better, but he started his jump a good half to three-quarters of a foot before the take off line—so that part wasn't measured. But I can remember seeing him land in a cloud of dust and get up with a spring in his step, knowing that that jump was something special.

Our class also "adopted" a Korean orphan through a United Nations program through which money was sent to the child's family in Korea to help provide necessities of life. We also collected good used clothing, about a ton (literally). I enjoyed working with both projects. And Don and I both worked on the yearbook.

Before I moved north, a long-time friend and I had made plans to go to teacher's college together. Then we were going to buy a Jeep, drive out to Nevada, and teach on an Indian reservation. (Doesn't that sound like a plan for two young teens?) I had told Don of my plans, but one evening, in my parent's kitchen, he asked me if I'd like to get married and raise my own tribe. When I told him yes, he smiled. When I told him I would like to have six children, his eyes got big!

After graduating together, we both worked for a year, and then were married. My parents had very kindly helped us to buy a small house in the city of Poughkeepsie—part of an estate, with some of the elderly couple's furniture in it (we still use the bedroom set)—instead of paying for a larger wedding. We enjoyed the little place. It was a quaint, Victorian-style house with a small front yard and backyard on a shady street with a brick walk separating us from the house next door. We painted and wallpapered, and loved every minute of it. Don also made a large decorative window box for outside the bay windows.

Our enjoyment was strengthened by Don's amazing patience. Even with red hair, he was, and still is, "not soon angry" (Titus 1:7), a trait I have always been thankful for, and which, though not by intention, I have tested a few times. I first saw this patience when he had been in the cellar shaking up a can of ceiling paint, not realizing the lid was not tight. He calmly called, "Can you come down here a minute?" His call was so calm that I was absolutely thunderstruck to find his face completely covered in white paint—but he calmly wiped it off with the cloth I hurried to get him.

Not many days hence, he displayed that patience toward me. The wall of the bathroom followed the slant of the roof, and I absolutely astounded myself by cutting the slant in the wallpaper wrong—at least twice in a row, and maybe even a third time. Don was pretty amazed too, but he never got angry. I think he realized that it wasn't something I enjoyed doing—even if I did do it more than once.

Back in the 1950s the dangers of smoking were not considered at all. Don's father smoked cigarettes, and Don didn't like them. As a young teen he hid a very small firecracker in one of the man's cigarettes, and after it blew he ran like the dickens. No harm was done, and fortunately his dad laughed at the prank. But soon after we were married, Don took up the pipe. We both liked the smell, and he worked at using one. The end came when we were stopped at a light in a nice residential street near our house, and noticed smoke curling up with increasing rapidity from the ashtray in the dash of the car. Don yanked the ash tray out, opened his door, and dumped the contents on the street. However, more than the ashes of his pipe had been in the ash tray. The knob to the window handle, coins, bolts, and nuts began rolling around with Don hanging out of the car trying to scrape it all up. He lost taste in the pipe after that and we've never missed it.

Many years later, Don caught one of our sons trying to smoke. As an adult, that son said he was so very grateful for the sound spanking his father gave him, for he was never, in any way, tempted to try it again. He said that spanking was a super deterrent, and he is so glad! (So are we!)

Another adjustment to marriage that was a bit difficult was learning to sleep with someone else in the bed. We had both been raised in twin beds, and one night, in the pitch dark, we rolled over—Don doesn't roll over, he lunges—and banged heads so hard you could have heard the crack at the end of the street. We both sat up rubbing our bumps, saying, "Are you all right?" "Yes, are you all right?"

Our little house was near a fire hall. Don worked from three o'clock to eleven o'clock in the evening, while I worked eight o'clock in the morning to four o'clock. One morning as I was getting my lunch ready, the seven o'clock fire horn—an ugly, raspy thing—went off. The young man upstairs called out from sleep, "I'll be right up!" Was that terrible noise what he thought I sounded like? I should have gone and hit him! (But of course I didn't—I just laughed.)

Then, the biggest adjustment: fright came when Don cut his hair. Don and his mom both had beautiful wavy red hair. In fact, my dear little grandmother cornered me in my mother's kitchen after my grandparents had met Don over a meal. "Irene," she said, "I hope that young man didn't notice—but I just couldn't keep my eyes off his hair!"

The fashion for long hair hadn't hit—so Don's hair was just average length. But in the middle of the first summer we were married, he decided to get a crew cut. It was Friday, and as usual he came down to the office where I worked to bring me home for lunch and then take me back. The car, a 1950 Chevy, had slanted windows on the side, so all I could see when I walked up to it was Don's broad smile. Imagine my surprise when I opened the door to get in, and he was nearly bald!

He went on to work in the afternoon, and I was already sound asleep when he got home. Thoughtfully, he went to bed without turning on the light. However, when I woke the next morning in the daylight, I was absolutely terrified! Don had his back to me, and I didn't recognize his head! Thankfully, I stifled a scream, which would also have been heard to the end of the street, and realized it was Don with his new "do." But the heart-thumping panic of thinking someone strange was in the bed—I can still feel it.

2

School and Work

WE BOTH CONTINUED working, but in the early fall, a friend named Bill, who was attending college and who had been Don's best man, invited us to come visit him at the technical college in a small town in western New York.

The guys were really close friends in high school. Don and Bill used to meet whenever possible in front of an old upright piano on the auditorium stage and play "rinky-tink"—Bill chording the bass and Don ad-libbing the top. They were good! And one of our friends put thumb tacks in the heads of the hammers, which gave it a more "tinny" sound. We all loved it!

One thing I forgot to mention: maybe two or three months after we were married, we bought a brand new 1955 VW Bug for $1,500. We put a down payment of close to $500—all in half dollars, which Don, his mom, and I had saved from the time wedding plans had seemed to be "in the wind." Needless to say, the car dealer was rather startled when Don carried into his office several coffee cans and a paper bag full of coins.

Don and I drove up to visit Bill in our little Bug, and the following fall drove up to our new home in the married students' housing with our first son, Donny Jr., approximately one month old, so Don could begin college. The home was an apartment in one of several old wooden army barracks; white clapboard and two stories tall, with eight apartments each. The apartments consisted of two bedrooms, a living room, a kitchen, and a bathroom with a shower (no tub). But they were cozy and warm, and the friendships among the other married students were even warmer. We were all pretty much in the same boat financially, and almost all of us had young children. And of course all the daddies had a lot of studies.

Don, because he had not made any provision in high school for further training, had to take a prep course to make up the math he needed, which would mean an extra year for us. He arranged his schedule to have only eight o'clock classes (the earliest offered), so he could be finished in time to babysit our little son when I went to work in one of the town restaurants from three o'clock to eleven o'clock at night. It was a gathering place for students during study breaks and served many of them meals. It was pleasant work, and the employees were busy almost all the time; so much so that when I finished in June and went on a picnic in July, I wore regular women's size twelve shorts and was six months along! Believe me, that was the only pregnancy that ever happened! For all of my other pregnancies, maternity clothes were my uniform after my fourth month.

One evening while babysitting as I worked, Don laid Donny on the little kitchen table while he scooted into the bedroom to get a diaper off the shelves he had built there. He kept his eye on the baby, and to his shock, Donny rolled over for the first time—right off the table.

Thankfully, Don's reflex action was amazing, and he scooped the baby up before he ever hit the floor! Don's arm hit the floor hard—enough to skin it pretty good from the elbow to the wrist, and the bang of his arm, then the baby's scream of fright, brought the neighbor lady from across the hall to see if the baby had been hurt. Thankfully, Donny was just fine and soon settled down to get his diaper changed and have his evening bottle. Even remembering that brings a big, "Whew, that was an extremely close one!" Needless to say, Daddy didn't trust the little guy to lie still again!

At Christmas, Don's folks kindly let us come and stay with them, and Don went to look for work. He got a job at the post office in Poughkeepsie, and with his let's-get-it-done attitude, was able to deliver about half again as much mail as they expected. Because of that, when he was standing in line with others hoping to be hired the following Christmas, he was recognized, called out of the line, and given a job.

Don had finished the prep course in March, and at that time, the school had begun building two large brick dorms, so he got a job working construction and loved it. He was in top shape from running track in high school, and now became even more energetic. In fact, when the alarm would sound in the morning at about six thirty, he would literally hop out of bed to shut it off, whistling and eager for the day. I can't say I shared his enthusiasm for rising so early; in fact, I used to wonder what on earth all the racket was about at the crack of dawn!

We really enjoyed college life that first year. We were both busy, but it was great. We were together, on our own, and working together for something that would be beneficial in later years. We enjoyed fixing up the apartment—the school supplied the paint, a choice of about five pastels, with the stipulation that the ceiling be white—and using our second-hand furniture. The only new thing we had was a wringer-washer, given as a wedding present by Don's parents, and I hung my clothes from our kitchen window on a huge pulley line attached to the apartment building below us called the "T."

Two things come to mind when mentioning the laundry. One morning in the winter, I was busy hanging wash on the pulley line out the window. Don came into the living room to go back to his desk, and I popped my head back into the kitchen to say hello. At that very moment, a huge hunk of ice, about the size of a recliner, came rushing down with a loud thunderous *WHOOOSH!* right in front of the kitchen window I had been hanging clothes out of! If I had not, at that very instant, been inside, the ice would have taken off my head, literally.

The second memory is a bit funnier. One day, as Don was at his desk, his merciful quality was again exhibited. I washed his good watch in the washing machine, and only discovered it when I heard a noise as it went through the wringer in the pocket of his pants. He never got angry; my cry of "Oh, honey, I'm so sorry!" when I held up his watch must have let him know how very badly I felt. And he has never reminded me of it, either.

We had a very happy year, and the spring and summer were beautiful. We did have one adventure, however. Our neighbors were following our little Bug to a park for a picnic when they noticed excessive smoke coming from it. Sure enough, the engine was on fire. They signaled us to stop, and soon we stood grabbing handfuls of sand and throwing them on the engine, while the flames shot out at us. When it was over, all the wiring was burned away and of course the car wouldn't start. So we climbed in with our friends and went on and had our picnic. Another neighbor kindly towed the car back a few days later. And all the repair work only came to $25. We were amazed, but that man, Mr. Stevens of Alfred Station, was known for his honesty.

After the construction job was finished, Don sought odd jobs: trimming a professor's tree (Don fell and broke a couple of fingers) and scrubbing down a lady's kitchen (he was amazed at how greasy it was!). Don always took his responsibility to provide for us very seriously!

In the fall, Don's schedule picked up considerably. For that reason, he was unable to work, but had been given a job by the construction boss, who appreciated his diligence and his "a day's work for a day's pay" attitude. His job was to light the caution flares set up over the holes around the construction sites. That brought in a little income, and by budgeting and shopping once a month for groceries regardless of what we ran out of (powdered sugar in coffee isn't too bad), we made it through the year. We had been able to rent out our little home, which paid for its mortgage and our very cheap apartment rent. And that fall, we were blessed with a little daughter, Laura Ann. After that I could no longer waitress, for two little ones were too much for Don to care for while pursuing his studies.

But the long hours of homework every night until one or two o'clock in the morning, rising for an eight o'clock class, and studying all day Saturday and all day Sunday—along with a diet not so very rich in protein—took its toll on Don. Don was not the student type, so he had to work for what he got. The course he was taking, mechanical technology, was one of the toughest offered. Also, he had a questioning nature with a built-in why?—faced with a formula or problem that was supposed to work a certain way, he wanted to dig in and find out the background. And something I've always admired him for is that he was, and still is, scrupulously honest. Don never cheated in any way and to my way of thinking, that is a priceless legacy to give our children. His marks were only his!

At the close of school in the spring, Don went back to the construction job, got wet and chilled, contracted a cold, and wound up with pneumonia. Donny Jr. had by then developed the habit of eating mud. He would eat it every chance he got—the blacker, the better. Needless to say, this terribly upset me. The roughage caused diarrhea, which I tried to treat at home by carefully following our family doctor's advice, but I just couldn't imagine what was wrong. Don and I were both distressed about it and tried everything our doctor suggested, but to no avail. We were frantic. Finally, after several agonizing months, I took him to a pediatrician in a larger town. Just before our doctor visit, a neighbor's mother had said, "That child is low on iron," so I asked the pediatrician to check for that and also to treat his ear, which had begun to run with infection after a bout with measles. He did both, and poor little Donny had to have a series of eight intramuscular iron shots, one a day in his little bottom. Don was in bed with pneumonia, so it meant I had to drive—which I was new at and absolutely terrified of!—the little guy to the doctor's for eight days straight. He and I both dreaded the trips.

The doctor told Don he had to rest, so we called his folks to ask if we could come home for him to recuperate. They were very kind, and we spent time there until Don was on his feet. When we came back, he again got his construction job, this time on pick and shovel. He was doing fine until he decided to take the last two antibiotic tablets given him for pneumonia after a lapse of a few days from the main dosage. He then began diarrhea so badly he was even bleeding, though he still continued to work. Finally, giving in, he let me call the doctor who prescribed other medication, and he said the antibiotic tablet had killed the natural bacteria of his intestines, causing the problem. Don still worked, though very thin and weakened, and I can still remember the sick feeling I felt when I would bring him his lunch, hear the dull thud of the pick, and know what it was costing him physically to swing it.

The third year his schedule was even heavier, and there was no lamp-tending job to keep, as there were no holes that need the caution flares anymore. We had saved a little in the summer to take care of the tuition and books, and our little house was still rented out, but groceries were another thing! It was impossible for Don to work and also have any time at all to sleep. He was carrying thirty-one class hours most semesters, with the lightest semester being twenty-six class hours. Often he ate his supper right at his desk rather than leave his studies. For this reason, I had to become the breadwinner somehow.

I began to sell Avon, a cosmetics line; enjoyed it, made out fairly well, and even won some awards for selling the most in certain time periods. What I brought in from Avon sales determined what money we had for buying groceries. This, of course, gave me an incentive to go out every evening after Don and the children had eaten supper and the little ones were tucked into bed. Many times I stumbled through snow up to a door in the dark to knock and present my wares.

In fact, one February night I knocked on a door only to have the elderly lady woman inside say in surprise, "What are you doing out there? It's nineteen degrees below zero! Come in and get warm by the fire!" As I remember she didn't buy anything—but I was glad for a few moments of warmth, though I remember the push inside me to keep going. Memories of those night-time selling trips are the reason we always have kept our porch light on, to help someone who may have a need. Through the years, we have been blessed to be available by our light.

By the way, I did this all through my third pregnancy. By the middle of February, I couldn't go out any longer, and a friend kindly sold for me awhile, which helped a little. Our precious third child—another son, David Allen—was born March 8. And from the week I brought him home, until the week of Don's graduation at the end of May, the only meat we had was one pound of hamburger for the entire family, and I was nursing the baby. Our diet consisted mostly of casseroles, but not too long after supper it seemed there would be a craving for something to stay with you. It was during this time that Don and I felt we could understand and identify just a little with those in the "have-not" nations, with one exception: we knew that there would be a change after graduation. How heartbreaking it must be to have a family and know there is no chance of anything better than a "just making it" diet, or worse. A poor diet really does affect one, and it would be a good thing if making good eating choices could be taught and even stressed in schools.

3

We Found What Had Been Missing

AFTER THE BABY was born, a dramatic event occurred in our lives. It was through my selling that we entered into a whole new area of life. One of my customers told me that we could know and have God as our Father (not just in the Creator Father sense) through accepting the forgiveness of our sins offered by Jesus Christ as the Bible teaches. I didn't want to listen, but because of her precious kindness—giving us her son's outgrown clothes, and even food—we wanted to somehow try to repay her. Knowing her love for the little church group that met in the town, pastored early Sunday mornings by Rev. Alton Shea (brother of George "Bev" Shea, the singer with Billy Graham), who then drove back to preach at his own church in Wellsville, we decided to ask if they would christen our baby.

Pastor Shea sent word that he wanted to come to the house to see us. With the pastor coming, I scurried around to have our little place just spotless. Of course, my two little friends didn't have the same vision, and as fast as I could get the books tidied on the shelf, they would pull them down. I began to fuss, and I'm sure the volume wasn't very pleasant. At that very moment, there was a knock.

Of Pastor Shea, my friend had told me that "he radiates love." I had thought "Yeah, sure!"

When I opened the door, Pastor Shea said, "Why, you have *three* precious little ones!" I felt that God had slapped my face, even though the pastor's voice was very gentle and kind! I thought, "They really are precious, and I'm yelling at them!" I was greatly ashamed before God.

Discipline means training—for the good of the recipient—not a means to lower the steam-pressure in the trainer! The Bible even speaks of the "rod of correction" in terms of dealing with children. (See Proverbs 22:15.) And the beloved Psalm 23 speaks of the Shepherd's rod bringing comfort. A child finds the comfort of security when there are boundaries with consequences. They may act like they want to run things—but deep inside they want to know someone else is in charge. And when we really put our trust in the Lord over a matter, don't we also then find peace? But He never deals with us in anger, and we should not ever discipline in anger. I must admit, I've failed there, but my heart was to not do so.

After Pastor was seated, Don joined us. Instead of explaining the order of the ritual of the christening service as we had supposed he would, he told us it was necessary to acknowledge that Christ's death was to pay for our sins too, and we needed to make a personal commitment of our lives to Him to be sure of heaven. This we did, though not understanding fully what it meant. But we both prayed sincerely and gave ourselves to Jesus.

Growing up, I had been a mild rather than a wild girl. I never drank or smoked and intensely disliked dirty jokes and that kind of conversation. This was largely due to my love and respect for my grandfather, who would have been deeply hurt if those things had been in my lifestyle. Because of this, I thought I was OK for heaven. (How blind can one be?) However, when our first two children were christened (a ritual of my parents' church), I wept very deeply at each ceremony, realizing that there was a new little life in my hands! Not only was I supposed to guide them to do right, but also to make them *want* inwardly to *do* right! I felt so completely helpless!

But God is so kind, and the way He helped me realize that something had actually happened was that at the christening service—which Pastor Shea kindly performed though it was not a part of their church beliefs—I felt only deep joy, because for some strange reason I felt I could actually ask God for help!

To explain for just a moment, giving one's life to Jesus by acknowledging that His death was for one's own sins too, moves an individual from being a loved creation of God, to a beloved child of God: a big difference! After an individual does that, he or she should be baptized—as Jesus Himself was—though it is a choice made by the one who has surrendered to Christ. For that reason, some churches present the babies to the Lord in a dedication ceremony as the baby Jesus was presented in the temple, and omit the christening part, which symbolizes baptism. The bottom line is that we give our lives to Jesus, and then as parents commit ourselves by example and teaching to lead our precious children to come to know and love Jesus Christ. What an amazing difference it makes in a home!

Before I go on, there are a couple of little adventures we had in the Heights—or "Diaper Hill," as the housing complex was called—that I don't want to forget to mention. Donny Jr. realized that if he got up very early and moved really quietly, he could do stuff. Early, early one morning, after we had gotten groceries the evening before, Donny must have "heard" dawn break, and tip-toed out while Dad and Mom were sleeping. When we got up, we found a tall white cone, about three feet high, of all the powdered things we had bought the evening before.

There was laundry powder, powdered milk, granulated sugar, powdered sugar, cornstarch, and more. Our little friend had had himself quite a time. There really wasn't a mess—but a definite mountain of powder coming to quite a point. The cone was quite an impressive creation, considering the builder had recently just turned two years old! We were rather surprised. Thankfully, this was when Don was still working construction and we had a little more money.

We wanted to take an Easter picture of the three little ones, but there was one hitch. We only had three shots left on our little camera, and of course no extra money to get another roll of film. Carefully we put a baby blanket over the back of the little couch we had had re-upholstered, to make a nice background that the children could sit on. We lined them up, me trying to have everyone smile, and Don manning the camera. In the middle of the first shot, the baby—probably one month old—started to cry. During the second, he fell over on his side.

Finally, there was peace. Everyone was in place, looking in our direction. But the very moment Don pushed the camera button, Donny Jr. opened his mouth so wide it was amazing! As for a picture, the expression on Don's face was also amazing! He was absolutely stunned, and I wish I had a shot of that!

I'd like to share a few more cute and sweet memories that are too precious to leave out. When we first went to college,

Donny Jr. was only about one month old. Don's friend Rudy—the one who "chorded" the piano in high school and who was Don's best man and a big influence in Don attending college—came to visit us in our little apartment. To answer Rudy's question about the baby, Don said, "You should see my son in his bassinet, flexing his biceps!" So I began to sing a little song to the baby to the tune of "You're My Honey-Love." The words were: "You're a muscle-man, a little ba-bee muscle-man. Da-dee-da, dee-da-dee. Da-de-dum-dum," et cetera. The last part went, "I know he loves me, I know he loves me, because he says so. He is my little baby sweetie. He is my baby muscle-man."

Our little daughter Laura really enjoyed her bottles. I used to sing her a song to the tune of the car advertisement song, "Wouldn't You Really Rather Have a Buick?" The words went, "Wouldn't you really rather have a bottle, a bottle, a bottle? Wouldn't you really rather have a bottle, than any other thing at all?" When I started to sing that, she knew a treat was coming! One time she was standing in her crib, and as soon as I handed her the bottle she just let herself fall backwards! Eeek! To be sure, the next time I handed her the bottle, I cradled her with my arm!

4

Back From College

AFTER GRADUATION, DON went back to Poughkeepsie and IBM to work, this time in the Apprentice Toolmaking School. We moved into a small rented house, and began to learn about suburban life and God. For one thing, we learned He does answer prayer, sometimes in the most unusual way.

I had been sickened and dismayed by a thought that kept coming to mind. "Isn't it conceited for God to want someone to worship Him?" The thought would come in a cynical, scorning tone, almost if something were sitting on my shoulder, speaking into my ear. I would apologize to God over and over and prayed that the thought would be removed. Not too long after, our baby David, ten months old, became seriously infected and swollen in his male organs, so much so that the doctor warned surgery might be necessary which would prevent him from ever becoming a father. After three days of extremely strong medication, which could not be continued any longer than that, he was no better and screamed as I diapered him for bed the fourth night, gently pinning the diaper on each side.

Contemplation of what might be coming had exhausted Don and I, though the night before, after reading Luke 18:2–8, we had prayed for God's help for our baby. As we sat limply in the living room staring blankly at each other, the phone rang. It was the doctor, asking to see the baby in his office because a friend, a urologist, was visiting him and wanted to see the little one. When I undressed the child there—two hours after putting him to bed, sick, feverish, and in pain—the doctor, his friend the urologist, and I were completely thunderstruck to see the baby was perfectly and completely healed! Though he had screamed in pain as I pinned the diaper on the sides, he lay peacefully without a whimper as the urologist carefully examined him. "There is nothing wrong with this baby!" he said. His exam was so thorough that he even caused a little bleeding, but David just laid there peacefully and looked at him! Needless to say, no longer did I question why God should be worshiped, and I never heard that phrase in my mind again, ever!

We had a couple of little adventures while at the little house. For one, Donny, age three, found a pair of small scissors outside that had been left by the family before us. For some reason he decided to give his sister, not quite two, a haircut on the top of her head. It was so close to the scalp that when you patted her dear little head, you felt stubble—as if she had a crew cut!

The little house had a small garage, and in it, on the side under a little wooden coffin-shaped box, was the pump over the well. To Donny, it was an "engine," and of course, *all* engines need gasoline. Don had left a container of gas out as he had been working on our car.

Busy in the house, with periodic checks on the children, I had no idea that during one of the intervals Donny had poured gasoline into the pump, and therefore on into the well! The news broke that evening when Don took a shower after work, and was coughing because of the gasoline fumes. Life has never been dull!

Christmas gave us a phrase that has brought chuckles to our family forever. My parents and my petite grandmother, my father's mother, came to our little house for Christmas morning with our three tykes. Don was on his side, reaching way under to the back of the tree to retrieve a gift. Suddenly the tree began to totter, and in spite of all the adults lunging to grab it, down it came on Don's back.

In a few minutes the tree was secured, and Don crawled out from under. His first words were, "Did much fall off?" and we all folded in laughter. That phrase has eased tensions and brought smiles as the dust settled after various crashes along the road of our lives.

During that time, I became pregnant, but after about five months, complications set in. I was ordered to bed. Our folks kindly helped with the children, and the church folks brought meals and were such a help. I remember being so touched and amazed that one of the church ladies—who was quite wealthy—was the one to do our laundry.

One evening the little one, a boy, came. I remember holding him in my hand, and he was about that big, stillborn. I had then to go to the hospital for a procedure, and they kept me that night in the maternity wing. It was extremely difficult to hear the babies crying and know that my arms would be empty. My heart goes out to women who have lost a little one. It really is heartbreaking.

Years and years later—when our David was a senior in high school—he shared a bedroom with his brother Daniel (the next one in the line). When I came to wake them for school, he said, "Mom, do you know what we were just talking about? We were wondering what it would have been like if we had that other Daniel too."

My heart sang! Apparently they didn't feel as if they were lost in a mob—they knew that each one was precious and valuable! What a sweet joy to me!

After the baby boy whom King David had with Bathsheba died (2 Samuel 12:18–21), the king said, "I will go to him, but he will not return to me" (2 Samuel 12:23, NIV). So I know that some day I will see our little one. In the process of time, I did have two more miscarriages—none as far along as the first. I had three names picked out—Dennis Matthew, Dwight Nathaniel, and Loretta Faith—and you know, I feel I will meet them "up there." The Lord is so kind, and I believe what King David said teaches that the Lord receives little ones—no matter how they come. What beautiful hope He gives!

A Second Touch From God

We moved back into our own little house after the tenants moved out, and our feeling of not belonging and our yearning for the college town (a yearning which had begun before we had even left after graduation) persisted. So, even though we were soon to have our fourth child, and Don had seniority, many benefits, and the promise of a lucrative job upon completion of his training at IBM, we decided to once again head westward to college, if at all possible, that coming fall.

In the spring our faith was tested, or rather shored up, when labor began prematurely for the baby, who was in the breech position. God wonderfully delivered both of us from the "valley of the shadow" (Ps. 23:4).

Labor began Saturday evening, and on Sunday morning Don called the church we were attending to ask for prayer because the doctor had told him that both the unborn baby and I were not doing very well at all and that both of us could be lost. Two members came over to pray with him in the father's waiting room. As they were kneeling in prayer, Don felt impelled to raise his head and open his eyes—and found himself looking at a wall clock which read nine thirty in the morning. A short time after that, the doctor came to him and said, "I don't understand it! Things were getting worse and suddenly, at nine thirty—two contractions and the baby was born! He is just fine and so is your wife!"

For my part, I can remember being on the delivery table and being desperately tired. Things began to get dark. I heard a tense voice say, "Give her oxygen!" But I was so very tired, too tired to even take a breath. And I heard someone say tersely, "Breathe!"—but I barely could. It was at that point the two contractions came and our precious little son, Daniel Thomas, our fourth child, was born. I can still remember seeing his dear little face looking over at me from the newborn bed they placed him into before he was weighed. And I felt super, full of energy and exuberance. Afterwards, several people came to my hospital room, nurses and others, who told me of hearing how bad things were going during the delivery, and how surprised they were with the outcome. They also were amazed to see me so energetic and joyful! And what a joy it was to tell them the Lord was the reason!

The summer sped along, the baby grew, and the neighborhood children "found" us. It was fun to have them around, and they really did want to help. I felt badly when one of the young girls burned an iron-shaped hole in the swim trunks Don wore on our honeymoon while she was helping one day.

The dismay on her face was enough that I gave her comfort rather than a rebuke. When our church had vacation Bible school, the gang of children accompanied me and the baby carriage there every day. The children were enthusiastic and enjoyed it, and the church folks and I were grateful.

One funny thing happened which requires that I tell on our second son, probably not to his pleasure. (But I really love him. He is super!) Gramma and Grampa Burns had come to see the family one evening and brought a great big Hershey's chocolate bar. Because it was near bedtime, I only allowed the children to have one or two small pieces. When the folks left, we all tucked ourselves into bed. But the memory of the treat opened a pair of little eyes bright and early. He tiptoed downstairs and devoured almost all of the chocolate bar. But his poor little tummy couldn't handle all that rich food. His little intestines began to function—in the front hall, on the front porch, down the walk, and finally on the running board of the neighbor's car! I found out about the final resting place as I was following (and cleaning up) the trail; the neighbor yelled out irately, "Did you see what your kid did to my car!" as he was hosing down his automobile!

Believe me, I hadn't slept in. When you have four alarm clocks—one being a small baby—you don't. But I can see the Lord's hand of mercy upon the little guy. Never a dull moment—especially with him!

One day he came down the steps, carrying his baby brother! That was quite a feat since he had turned two in March and his brother, born in late May, was at that time about three months old. He explained, "The baby was crying."

He has always been very strong. Not long after that, after I settled his older brother and sister in for their naps, I called to him to come so I could put him into his crib. He came running full tilt, grabbed the crib rail and did a flip, landing with a bounce on the mattress. I almost had a heart attack!

Don's father and brother were managers at IBM and the door that led in that direction was the Apprentice Toolmaker's School. Though Don was doing well in it, he did not enjoy it at all. A big part of that lack of enjoyment was missing the slower pace of life in the rural area where he had gone to college. I shared that feeling.

To try to pacify both sets of parents, Don decided to go back to college. It offered an excuse to leave the secure and promising position he was in. Both sets of parents, but especially my father, were understandably concerned that we be financially secure. Therefore, going back for additional training instead of just leaving the factory and all the benefits it offered showed that other doors of opportunity could open for him. This eased the worry a bit. When Don told me his decision, I was very grateful.

The day he left IBM and shook hands with his fellow workers, Don told me that one of the men said, "I wish *my* wife would let me do that!" Again, I was so grateful not to have opposed his decision. No matter what the financial provision would have been, if he was unhappy, it wouldn't have been worth it. And besides—who wants to live in a rut? Adventure, anyone?

5

We Take the Leap

FALL WAS FAST approaching, so Don made arrangements to enter school in September. However, the little house had not been sold, nor were there any inquiries. The afternoon before he was to leave, I was working up in one of the bedrooms, and knelt to pray about the situation. As I prayed, it felt as if a heavy weight was lifted off my back, and that evening as I was ironing and packing Don's clothes, I told Don's dad I knew that the house would be sold. He asked how I knew, and I told him about the weight being lifted.

Don left the next morning to drive the 280 miles in our 1954 Rambler, with water squirting out of its exhaust. On the way up he had to stop at a garage, and when the attendant took a compression test, he was startled to find a cylinder filled with water! But Don made it, and the very afternoon of his departure an elderly gentleman who owned a tourist home down the street, but was retiring, took a stroll past our house, saw the sign, looked the place over, and bought it. I was absolutely amazed!

It took about a month to get the papers signed and get things packed and ready. Don stayed up at school, readied our apartment—the same one as before—built bunk beds, and read his Bible. He was much more at peace when he came to move us, and even his face looked different, with an inner strength and peace quite noticeable. God's Word does amazing things.

We moved our little gang back into the two-bedroom apartment with the baby in the crib, two feet-to-feet on the bottom bunk, and Don Jr. on the top. Don was able to obtain credit for several courses, so his schedule was not anywhere near as heavy as before, and the course of study itself, building construction, was not as taxing, so he was able to work a bit at odd jobs. We were very happy and busy, and were enjoying the people around us.

Soon after settling in, we met a family from Baltimore who had also recently committed their lives to Christ. The husband was in the graduate school for engineering at the university, and they had five children. It wasn't too long after they settled in that a Bible study started in their home as a result of sharing their faith with a young married couple. Many of us spent many precious hours together around God's Word, and the Bible study continued on Friday evenings for many, many years.

Their children and ours became close friends, and that brought a few adventures—especially thanks to our son and their son, both named David.

One day I heard a rumble in the yard and ran to the front window. To my amazement, the two Davids were diving over the big, empty galvanized trashcans as they rolled them down the little hill of the yard in the front of our building! Then there was the time they accidentally set the woods across from the other David's house on fire! Between our David and our friend's son David, things were never dull! (It must be something about the name!)

Another source of real joy was the Japanese family that moved in next to us in our building. The husband was a brilliant research scientist and spoke English. His wife, sweet and very gifted, and their two sons, ages twelve and seven, did not speak English at all. The manager of The Heights, the housing project, asked us to help them adjust and get acquainted, and it was such a privilege to learn to communicate with them, to learn about their life in Japan (both boys had been chosen to go to a school for exceptional children), and even to learn how to cook some delicious and helpful dishes that I still serve today.

I would take the Japanese woman grocery shopping, as she learned to drive sometime later, and often bought something so she could taste it (for instance, she had never had brown sugar in Japan). I really loved her, and it was a joy to share a few of my family's things to help her keep house, like our "cleaning machine" (vacuum cleaner) and our sewing machine. Her gentleness and talent were such an inspiration, and it was really great to find that our language barrier wasn't a barrier at all.

Her boys fit right in and seemed to enjoy themselves. The oldest actually skipped a grade, even though at the start he spoke no English! But he was all boy, and I saw his brother and him one summer afternoon rolling on the ground, convulsed with laughter, when they happened to see Don Jr., age six, whiz out the kitchen window on the clothesline and let himself down to the ground. Needless to say, I too was a bit startled with the acrobatic act!

That spring, Don's family graciously allowed us to bring them down to Poughkeepsie for a visit. Grampa and Gramma kindly kept the children and allowed us to take the Iida family, our Japanese neighbors, to New York City to sightsee!

It was a wonderful time! Don also taught Dr. Iida how to drive our little Bug. There were a few harrowing experiences, but all ended well. We really loved them, and that summer Don helped them move to New Jersey, where Dr. Iida would continue his studies.

When they left early the next morning, I remember getting down on my knees in front of our little heater and praying—almost with a deep physical ache—that they would somehow find Jesus. Though we tried, we just couldn't reach them. I remember trying to explain salvation on the way home from a ladies' meeting at our church, and Yokiko replying with broken English, "I just a little bit Buddhist." I knew that because of the language barrier, she really hadn't understood much that had been said at the meeting, and I was very thankful that she had even come with me.

A year or two went by, and we lost contact with them. About that time, Billy Graham held a crusade in Kyoto, Japan—their city. We had been getting his *Decision* magazine—a shiny newsmagazine, and there, on the front page, was a large picture of two Japanese boys sitting and being counseled after they had given their lives to Christ in the Crusade. We were astonished and overjoyed to recognize the two boys as Akio and Nobo, the very ones who had been our neighbors! Truly, the Lord is so very kind!

It's hard to condense two years of living into writing. Many things happened that are now fond memories. Don's only sibling is an older brother, so when our first daughter, Laura, came along, he was so pleased. He enjoyed her being dressed in ruffles, which I was happy to do. I starched and ironed her little dresses and petticoats, and she even owned several pairs of tights with ruffles across the bottom. She really looked so sweet. One thing that was especially cute was her little nose. It wiggled when she would talk and was just adorable to watch.

One day, Don was laying on the couch and had Laura sitting up on his chest. He said, "Sing to me, Laura," so in her squeaky little voice, so sincerely, she sang: "Jesus loves the little children, all the children of the world. Red and yellow, black and…green…they are precious in His sight." Don almost choked not to laugh! "Sing it again, honey," he said. (Wouldn't you have asked for an encore?)

Just a year or two later, while looking out the window at the landscape, that same little voice spoke up from the back seat of the car—again, so sincere. "Mommy, don't you wish the *whole world* was pink?" A few years later her little sister, while riding in the car on the same road, piped up from the back, "Mommy, don't you wish the snow was purple?" (Must have been something about that road!)

One time Laura and David were at the little kitchen table. The subject of David's strength came up.

"You're not very strong!" said Laura.

"Oh yes I am!"

"No you're not!"

"I am so!"

"I bet you can't pick up this house!"

And would you believe they both got down and bustled out to the little front porch of the apartment building to try his strength! Sometimes our duties and busyness rob us of precious moments. I can't for the life of me remember what I was doing at the time, but I know this—I really regret that I didn't stop and peek out the window to watch!

Of course, our budget was a bit tight, so one time we called Don's mom for her birthday on the phone of the folks upstairs—with arrangements to pay them for the call. His mom was a very sweet and gentle lady, and I knew she would enjoy hearing her grandchildren sing "Happy Birthday." They stood in a row (cute as could be, of course!) and all sang very sincerely. I passed the phone along the line, letting each little voice be heard.

To my amazement, when I got to David, he was singing with his deep little voice from the heart, "Mody Gaddy to you!" Mody Gaddy? Where in the world did he ever get that? Thankfully his brother and sister didn't notice, and I was able to choke back my laughter. But things like that are such fun to remember!

One time Don Jr. won a baby chick at the town Easter party. That evening after the children were settled and Don and I were sitting at the little kitchen table having a cup of tea, the baby chick kept trying to jump into our laps. The next day, when Don went to the school poultry farm to buy eggs, he told the man about it. The person said the chick was lonely, but that state law prohibited him from selling just one chick.

I was laying on the couch (which I didn't do often!) fighting a "bug" of some sort, when Don came home with a bag of feed in one hand and a suspicious-looking bag that moved in the other. He had bought the minimum allowance—six more chicks. Don built a low box-pen, and we kept it in the children's bedroom—the only place big enough. Later, when the chicks began to hop out, he added a mesh top. We kept the chicks in our apartment for two months, and I think the building manager was conveniently oblivious to the whole thing. We did, however, get a bit nervous when the roosters began to practice crowing.

And there was the winter day I rolled our VW bus over, with no injuries. A few weeks later it was rear-ended, and we were given $500 by the other driver's insurance company, to our amazement. We were even more amazed when, the day after we tithed the check—a little reluctantly, I'm ashamed to say—we received a check for $50 from the people at the church in Poughkeepsie who were "thinking about us," along with some lovely clothes for the children. Again, God was telling us He was there!

When we came back to college, the little church that met in the chapel was no longer meeting, so we went to a small church of the same denomination as the one we had been attending in Poughkeepsie, in a small, nearby city. I'll never forget the adult Sunday School teacher's comment that even in our trials, we'll never know what the Lord spared us from.

The truth of that comment was very real to us, because the spring before our move back to school, we had decided to visit Don's best friend Rudy and his wife in Rochester. We loaded the little gang into our VW Beetle, all of them comfortable on the setup Don had made which turned the entire back seat into a bed, right up to the backs of the front seats.

About three-quarters of the way there, we developed engine trouble, and Don had to call a tow truck. Don then rode with the driver, and I stayed in our little car with the children, who were sleeping. When the tow truck stopped for gas and to get information for Don about where a VW repair shop might be, I scooted out to powder my nose. To my shock, when I came out of the ladies' room, the tow truck and our car were gone! I stood for a few moments rather stunned, wondering what to do, when sure enough, back they came.

Whew! Don said he had looked back to make sure the car was okay and found no wife!

The tow truck driver took us to a place that kindly allowed Don to do his own work on the engine. We had prayed for the Lord's help, and he was able to improvise with some odd parts and get the lil' critter on the road again! We were very grateful, and the Lord reminded me of this incident with the Sunday school teacher's statement, "We'll never know what the Lord spared us from."

A dear little elderly lady who lived in the college town, and visited (and I'm sure prayed for) us in The Heights, went to our little church. Don very kindly let me go to prayer meeting with her, in her little 1949 Plymouth with two other ladies, on Wednesday evenings. (That meant he would have to bed down four little people—so it was really sweet of him.)

One evening as we were driving along, we came up to a car weaving along, going in the same direction as us. Our little friend pulled up alongside of it to look at the driver! She was not a bit aware that a car was coming at us in the lane she had driven into!

That car must have driven onto the shoulder of the road and passed us, but I didn't see a thing. I had my eyes tightly closed, and honestly thought I was going to enter heaven. When she passed the drunk driver and got back into the lane ahead of him, she said to us, "Did you see his *face*?" Her driving was a bit notorious. An elder of the little church once remarked, "I'd rather meet the devil coming down the road than... [our little friend]."

We enjoyed the little church, took part in the Christmas program, and helped with Vacation Bible School. That was a frightening experience for me, for I was asked to head it up. Making banners and planning was fine—but having to lead the opening in front of more than seventy people was quite intimidating.

There were two ladies who provided the piano music for the songs on different evenings. One dear lady would look to me for cues to start a song with a look of deep concern on her face. This, of course, did nothing but increase my insecurity, which was pretty intense already. The other dear lady would look at me with a beautiful, beaming smile. It brought such a sweet peace, and much-needed confidence. It was a real lesson to me, and I've tried to incorporate it into my life.

The Bible school seemed to be a success, and we gave the children a little parchment-like scroll as a memento with this inscription:

- Say nothing you would not what to be found saying when Jesus comes.
- Do nothing you would not want to be found doing when Jesus comes.
- Go no place you would not want to be found in when Jesus comes.
- Jesus could come today!

How much more relevant is this today! That was *before* the Six-Day War! Now Jerusalem is under Israeli control, and many other prophecies are being fulfilled. He is coming!

After graduation, The Heights were set to be torn down, so it was vital, though almost impossible, to find a place to move to in the area. We expressed our need at the little church, they prayed, and that very Sunday afternoon a man came to show us a small red farmhouse, with a chicken coop, that was to be our home for ten years, and that would see our family grow to eight children.

6

The Red House

THE HOUSE WE were shown was a quaint, small, barn-red farmhouse with white trim, about midway on a dirt road between two towns—four miles each way. It was in a little valley, or dale, with a wide open field across from us with a few little scrub apple trees and brush immediately across the road. One neighbor lived around a half mile to our right, up on a rather steep hill toward the town in which the children would go to school; the other was almost a mile away, on the left, also up a hill. In the front yard was a good-sized tree, with spreading branches, perfect for swings and climbing, and another tree was by the fence of the barnyard and near the road.

The landlord, a professor at a nearby university, had a huge silver barn and barnyard to the left of the house and yard. We had a good-sized front yard and a large backyard, part of which was later turned into a garden. The driveway was on the right, and it ended in front of an old, long, four-bay garage with a two-floor shed built on the end. The house had a front porch, a porch enclosed off the kitchen on the driveway side, and a small back porch.

We were greeted by a rather dismal interior—but we had permission and financial help to do some redecorating, and a large gray cat that our little three-year-old son named Catty. (What else?) My husband tore out the kitchen walls and insulated, and we wallpapered with a light perky print of old-fashioned clocks and tea pots, and bought some light blue ruffled curtains to go with it. The woodwork was white, and there was a chimney we painted bright enamel red with some paint we found down in the old dirt cellar. The stove pipe to the wood stove I cooked all our food on was inserted into that chimney, located in the middle of the side wall. During the process, the dear folks from the church came up on a Saturday to give us a wonderful helping hand and a delicious lunch.

As the wrecking ball was heading toward our campus apartment, we moved to the farm—hauling things over in our old Ford station wagon. We moved in late June, and in late July our fifth child, and second daughter was born, Linda Gail.

The house had a central living room with two small rooms on the driveway side. On the left was a large bedroom with a small one off of it, as well as the enclosed stairs to the three upstairs rooms. These upstairs rooms were really cold and, as we later found out, were absolutely unusable in the winter.

The living room was next to the kitchen, and the door mainly used to enter the house was the side door into the kitchen where the porch was enclosed. Don later built a closet on the porch so we could hang winter coats there instead of wondering what on earth to do with them in the kitchen. The bathroom was between the kitchen and smallest bedroom, and believe it or not the cellar door was in the bathroom!

I hope you'll forgive me for spending time giving you the layout, but that does play a part in some of the events, and to be honest, I really was (and still am) quite fond of the little place. (Wish I could take you all on a tour!) We didn't live there long before we had a couple of adventures—and both involved David, our third child, second son. Are you surprised?

The landlord had Don work on a part of the silver barn. David, then about four and a half years old, went over to watch. A frog attracted his attention, and when he leaned over the posthole to see, he toppled in head-first, his little arms pinned tightly to his sides and his head in the water. Don was busy on a ladder working, but by the mercy of God, he heard a strange noise, looked around, and saw David's feet sticking up out of the posthole. He jumped off the ladder and grabbed him out of the hole! Davey rested on his little bed for a while and then was as busy as ever.

One summer day, Davey and his brother Donny were exploring and discovered a barrel full of creosote, a liquid used to preserve wood, in which the landlord was soaking some fence-posts. Naturally, Donny dropped a rather large rock into the barrel to see how deep it was. Unfortunately, the creosote splashed into Donny's eyes, temporarily blinding him. Bless David's little heart, he grabbed Donny's hand and led him to the house calling to me that Donny had been hurt. Quickly I brought Donny into the bathroom and kept splashing water in his eyes. Later I made up a saline solution and soaked pads of paper napkins for him to hold on his eyes. Once again God's mercy was shown, and he had no ill effects.

The summer continued with its incidents and happenings. Those notorious chickens were very pleased with their large coop attached to the garage, and the freedom to roam over the yard keeping the bug population down to a minimum. However, twice I went running outside at three-year-old

Daniel's cry. Once I found him running, trying to hold up his little shorts that had popped a waist-string, with a large rooster chasing him and pecking at his poor little bottom! A few days later, his cry brought me to find him kneeling, face to the ground, with that rooster on his back pecking at his head! Needless to say, that chicken population stayed in the coop after that.

Don also decided that it would be a good idea to start thinning the coop population, since most of them were roosters, and the ones that weren't didn't have the vaguest idea what a chicken was famous for—namely, eggs. That decision caused a bit of apprehension on my part. "Just how does one get a chicken to look and act like the packaged kind one could buy at the store?" this city girl mused. Well, Don took care of the first step in the garage shed, then brought it into the kitchen to be put into the pot of hot water he had told me to get ready on the stove. This step loosens the feathers and could be called step two. The description of the next few steps will be omitted—but we did meet with success, and had a nice chicken dinner quite often.

Our kitchen stove was a real joy to me. It was a wood stove, white porcelain, with a shelf across the top, and a nice roomy oven. I really enjoyed cooking on that thing, and even got to the point where I could judge the oven temperature by sticking in my hand, like my mother-in-law told me her mother used to do. Our budget was so tight that any treats were homemade, and my specialty was home-made biscuits and oatmeal cookies.

One Saturday afternoon, Don came home, strode into the kitchen, and made an announcement as he stood in front of the refrigerator. "Kids, this is good!" he said emphatically, and proceeded to put a full teaspoon of freshly ground horseradish into his mouth with a flourish. A group of little people watched in amazement as Daddy's face turned bright red, tears began to stream down his face, and I honestly thought I could hear the steam whistling out of his ears. I didn't ask them, but I wonder if they wondered about Daddy's definition of "good!"

Sometimes the Lord shows you He has been working in your life. We had a small radio on top of the refrigerator, and one day there was a "hurry up and buy" commercial on. The gist was that if you bought a car, you could get a set of pots and pans, free! Honestly, I usually would have tried to figure out how we could take advantage of that deal. However, when the commercial finished, I felt such joyful freedom! I said to the children, "I'm *free*, sweeties! We don't have to worry about that!" It was a wonderful feeling, and I find that for the most part I am quite content with what I have and am willing to fix, sew, etc. to provide what is needed. It really has brought peace and joy to my life, and I'm so grateful the Lord released me from the bondage of "stuff" and of worrying, What will people think?

We tackled the living room next and painted the low ceiling, old wainscoting, and woodwork a crisp white. The wallpaper we chose was a colonial snowflake print on—would you believe?—a cheerful bright red background. And I enjoyed keeping the white Cape Cod curtains starched and pretty. At first, we heated with a pot-bellied, wood burning stove. While I'm mentioning the Cape Cod curtains—they were a bit of work to iron, for I would go carefully around each ruffle and the little ruffle above the stitching that attached it to the curtain body. It took some time to do this, so naturally I was a bit protective of them.

When the gang was given some water pistols, the word was, "Do not squirt the guns in the living room!" Well, one day when I came in from hanging the wash (it seems that was a frequent activity), there was a blazing water gun battle going on, you guessed it, in the living room! Thankfully, the Lord took away the yell in me, so I just asked for the biggest water weapon. I took it out on the kitchen porch, laid it on the floor, and hit it as hard as I could with one of my iron skillets.

It shattered, and the stillness in the living room was deafening. I just went into the kitchen, got busy doing dishes, and everyone went quietly outside. At supper there was no complaining, and I never brought it up, either. Sometimes actions are better than words. It sure is a lot better than strife!

I did try to keep the house clean, and every fall and spring I would do a major house cleaning. This always included washing down the ceiling, walls, and cabinets of the kitchen. I also would empty the cabinets, wipe the shelves, wash the dishes that were not often used, put them and the pantry supplies all back.

The first step, of course, was cleaning all the ashes out of the wood stove—even the fine ash that lay inside between the cooking surface and the oven top. That process caused the ash to get into the air a bit, so I wanted it over before the other cleaning began. The kitchen was easier to do without my little helpers—so after the family was all bedded down for the night, I cleaned the ashes and began the shelves.

One morning Don was startled when he came home from work to find me on a ladder scrubbing the kitchen ceiling. (I even mixed ammonia and Clorox once to clear off the smoke stains. Cough! *That* was not wise!) It was work, but I really enjoyed making and trying to keep our home a pleasant place to live, even though it was humble. My grandmother once said to me, "It is no sin to be poor, but there is no excuse to be dirty." I've never felt shamed into cleaning, but have just really liked the results, and they seem to help bring a feeling of peace to the home that makes the effort so worthwhile.

I don't really enjoy cleaning that much. It is work, after all. But I do want with all my heart to keep our home clean to bring honor to the Lord. It isn't, and never has been, lavish—but there has been, and is, a peace there I treasure.

7

Our First Winter in the Country

THE FIRST WINTER was very cold there, as the house was quite drafty. I remember going into the large bedroom where we had all the children bunked at first, to call them for school, and finding snow all around Donny's face on his pillow. It had drifted in through the cracks around the window, having been blown hard across the open field. The curtains in the living room also moved in the wind—even with the windows shut—and one bitter night sitting by the wood stove, rocking my baby, I found I could still see my breath.

One night, God showed us again that He "never slumbers or sleeps" (Ps. 121:4). It was a cold wintry night, and to keep the fire in the pot stove lasting longer, Don loaded it with hardwood knots (pieces of wood with large knots formed where branches grow in them). He is normally an extremely sound sleeper—but this night he awakened for apparently no reason in the middle of the night. When he walked out into the living room, he was shocked to find the whole pot stove a livid, fiery red. The knots, with more sap in them, burned much hotter than regular wood, and had created a potentially very dangerous situation. Fortunately, we had placed a sheet of hard asbestos behind the stove against the white wainscoting—but things were dangerously hot. Don opened the damper (a round disk inside the stovepipe which, when closed, prevents the heat from escaping up the chimney) to let the fire burn down more quickly, and stood watch. When the fire had died down to a safe level, he prepared to return to bed—but before he did, he opened his Bible and it fell open to Psalms 4:8: "I will both lay me down in peace, and sleep: for thou, LORD, only makest me dwell in safety." Understandably, Don was awed by the evidence of God's awareness of an insignificant little family off on a dirt road, and His loving watch over them.

Don had been working independently as a carpenter since graduation, and at one of the jobs the windows that were ordered came the wrong size, and the folks gave them to him. So that spring, with our landlord's permission, he enclosed and rebuilt the front porch, which had needed repair. That made a big difference the next winter and also made a lovely "play house" porch for the girls.

When I became pregnant with our fourth son, the sixth child, I began to have painful backaches. Also, we had a serious need for quilts for the beds. I had been given some heavy old drapes that were my grandmother's—cotton-lined, but not a style that fit our house, so I opened the hems and sewed them together, as they were a pretty red tapestry-type material, and sewed other material in the back to make a quilt. Other quilts followed, made by the same or a similar method, filled mostly with old drapes and covered with large pieces of cotton framed with several strips of colors that related until the desired size was attained. The bottom side was done similarly. The layers were tied together by yarn pulled through and knotted, or sewn by machine. They were heavy and warm, and when I finished one just before the baby came, I found that getting up and down from the living room floor—where I had spread them out, and crawled around on them to lay them out and pin them—then up to the sewing machine to sew them, had exercised away my backache!

One day the next two younger boys, David and Daniel, were home sick and in bed because of it. (If someone was too sick for school, they had to stay in bed.) When I went to check on them, I found they had gotten into the small paint cans Donny had found in the cellar and put on a shelf near his bed. They got the paint on themselves and on Donny's quilt. They were a mess—so I put them into the tub while I finished the dishes. When I went in to get them, I saw the paint from their hands had drifted off to the surface of the water, and from that had stuck to two little bottoms—each sported a turquoise stripe. It's things like that you don't forget and can smile at the memory. I still have a small pair of underwear with a little bit of turquoise paint on it.

The arrangement of the bathroom door being at the end of the counter of the sink brings to mind another story. Often I would put the three oldest boys—Donny, David and Daniel—in to "tub it up" while I finished supper dishes. The tub—one of those old ones with feet—had a marvelous sloping end. It didn't take the gang long to find out that it made a super-duper slide. (So we had our own water park preview!) Unfortunately the water would splash all over when a little bottom "hit bottom." Hearing all the activity, I'd call out, "Boys! Stop sliding!" It would stop for a moment or so—but when something is *that* much fun it's hard to listen. Finally, in desperation, I'd call out, "Who wants a spanking?" The answer made me choke back laughter, for each voice strongly volunteered a brother! What a bunch!

A little aside about the notorious bathtub. For some strange reason, I wanted a modern tub that had a side that went to the floor. We found a secondhand tub leaning against an old barn and bought it for fifteen dollars. A friend, a college professor, came to help Don one evening, and the old tub was taken out, the new one hooked up. I had taken the children with me to the store, or perhaps the laundromat, and when we got back, we found we had missed the action! You see, Don had pushed the old tub down the back porch steps, then hopped in and rode it down the snowy yard! We all were very sorry not to have seen *that*!

During this time, we had been going to a small church in a little village nearby. Before we had left Poughkeepsie, an elderly lady had asked me if we had family altar or devotions in our home. When I replied that we didn't know what that was, she explained that it was a time set aside where the family gathers to sing, pray, and learn more about the Lord, and gave me a wonderful little book, *Devotions for the Children's Hour* by Kenneth Taylor, which, thankfully, is back in print. It was a great help in teaching all of us of the wonderful love that brought Christ to Earth and ultimately the cross, and our responsibility toward God. It started a habit that was a blessing for many years, and I wonder if that dear lady had any idea how important her caring was to our lives.

One story I still remember from the book is one in which a little boy told his mother he would be willing to die to save his friends. "I believe you would, honey," the mother said, "but would you die for a million mosquitoes?" What a picture of Christ's love for us!

Some of the ladies of the church began to come to our home on the dirt road for a prayer meeting one afternoon each week. One time when I was kneeling, "great with child"—number six—our little four-year-old daughter got on me and rode me like a horse! I had a hard time choking back the laughter, but I'm sure none of the ladies saw me. (Kinda think the Lord might have chuckled, though!)

The folks in the church were so very nice—kind, gentle, thoughtful, caring—but as I read the Bible my heart was stirred. Where was the power? I used to read the Bible when I nursed my baby, and was particularly gripped by Exodus 14:15–16. Moses was at the Red Sea, the Egyptian army was chasing the Israelites at a frightening pace. When Moses stood at the Sea wondering what to do, the Lord said, "Why do you cry to me? Lift up thy rod and divide the sea!"

God didn't say *He* would divide the sea, but that *Moses* should! My heart kept hungering to see the Lord's power manifested.

We found the winters at the little red house, as I said before, pretty severe. There was a lot of snow and the wind would drive it forcefully across the roads. The snow plows would mound it up almost daily, and most of the winter we drove a good portion of the way to our house through a "tunnel" of snow—mounds higher than the car on both sides of the road. Several times during those winters our car quit, and Don was forced to walk four miles down the hill to pick up a ride on the highway to get to work. Several times he had to do this for an entire week, until he could work on the car on Saturday. Don really gave his all to provide for his family!

I became pregnant, and felt the cold greatly. One night I went to bed dressed for the weather with a pair of heavy wool socks, Don's bright red flannel pajama bottoms, my long flannel nightgown, and a heavy sweater.

When I got quietly back in bed after a bathroom trip, I was amazed to hear Don chirp out in the dark, "Good ol' purple potatoes!"

What on *Earth*! It was so funny, but I didn't want to laugh out loud and awaken him, so I tried to muffle it. But I was definitely "great with child," and the more I muffled, the more I shook, and so did the bed. It wasn't long before someone awoke and said, "What's wrong with you?" "Me? *I* didn't say such a crazy thing!" (Even now it makes me laugh—he spoke it so very cheerfully!) And I had never even known there *were* such things—let alone fed them to him!

Some Things We Learned From Our Children

My parents very kindly would send packages up to the children for Christmas. (With our budget, it was really a priceless help!) My dad enjoyed corresponding by cassette tape, so we would have the children say their thank-yous on our little recorder, and mail that tape to them. Don would interview each child, and let them talk about their gift. When he got to Linda—about four years old—he had her say thank you for her nice slinky toy (a long spring-like toy that "walks" down steps.) Then he asked, "And what did we do with the slinky?"

The quiet little voice said, "We untangled it."

Don lost it! He laughed so hard he couldn't talk. We sent the tape anyway, and my folks laughed, too. Memories are such fun!

Doug was almost two years old when our seventh child, our fifth son, Dale Jonathan was born. Doug (number six), like Daniel (number four), had been a difficult birth, Doug even being a bottom breech. So when I learned another was on the way, again fear pecked at my peace. Near the end of my pregnancy, a dear traveling Bible teacher, Brother John Landis, stopped by to visit us. As he was leaving, I mentioned my concern and he said, "Irene, I will pray that this is your easiest delivery." It was quite easy, the baby was born fifteen minutes after I entered the delivery room.

A little aside: When I went into the hospital, Laura, 11, was the mom of the house and our church family helped with Doug, who wasn't yet in school. Before I left, I had been careful to "keep up the wash" and have all the girls' dresses ironed and ready. I felt so badly for Laura when I came home to find she had worn only one dress all week—to save laundry. What a thoughtful little sweetie!

And speaking of clothes, when Linda was about four, she went through a time when she would go into her room, get into her neatly organized dresser, change her clothes, and come bouncing out to ask me, "How does this look?" She would do this four or five times in a row, and unfortunately, each garment was happily tossed in a pile on the floor. Finally, in desperation I'd say, "If you change your clothes one more time you are going to get a spanking!" Laura couldn't understand why I would say such a thing to her sister—until her own second daughter was about four or five.

One more little event with those two girls. For Laura's birthday in October, as a real splurge we took the family to a restaurant that specialized in smorgasbord! When we got there, of course everyone went to wash hands before we ate, and Linda was amazed at the beautiful "sparkly" ladies' room. So it seemed like every six mouthfuls, she wanted Laura or I to take her to the bathroom. Kids!

Dale is now a fine, tall college graduate, and has turned out to be the easiest on me emotionally. He is very sincere and absolutely honest. But when he was a baby, he was quite fussy and didn't eat well. A friend decided to take her sister to a Kathryn Kuhlman healing meeting in Pittsburg and invited several of us to go along. As I was nursing Dale, he went with me. After the service, I was standing in the back of the church with the baby, and a lady came up and asked had I brought the baby to be healed. When I said no, she said, "Well, you look for a change in him. No one can be in the presence of God and not be changed." How true that is! Dale began to eat much better, accepting soft foods, and was no longer fussy.

Along with this, I had heard teaching about what power our words have. So, instead of calling him Daley-Wailey out of frustration, I began to call him Daley-Blessing—or sometimes just "Blessing." And truly he has been a blessing in my life.

To illustrate this—when Dale was about nine or ten years old, he had helped his Dad for two full Saturdays to work on several carburetors for our car. As he sat down at the breakfast table the third Saturday, knowing he probably had more of the same ahead of him, he said, "Helping Dad work on the car takes a lot of your time, but you learn a lot." That was the only "complaint" he made.

He also came to the table one morning and greeted me with, "If you kill one mosquito, you will have killed one million, nine hundred thirty-nine thousand, seven hundred and eighty-three mosquitoes," and started to eat his oatmeal. The Lord has often reminded me of that: how a little act of caring—maybe even causing ourselves an inconvenience or effort can often benefit many!

The Lord has used that to remind me of the value of the attitude of caring—even doing something insignificant in our eyes is worth so much more than we may know.

Dale manifests that attitude in his life.

8

More Lessons Learned From Our Children

SOMEONE ONCE TOLD me that God can speak to us through our children, and here are two times I'll never forget. One Sunday evening I was getting the children ready to go to the evening church service. I was tired, and with struggling boots onto little feet, then mittens, and fastening and zipping and tying, my irritability was showing. Then quietly, little three-and-a-half-years-old Daniel, pointing to a plaque over the kitchen sink, asked, "Mommy, what does that say?" Shamed, I read to him, "Jesus never fails." My irritability vanished, and it was a humbled and a much more peaceful Mom who went to church that evening.

Daniel's sensitivity to the Lord proved to be a protection for him when he was in kindergarten. The children were always clean and wore clean clothes, even though we passed them down as they were outgrown. In order to help a pair of hand-me-down jeans go a little farther, I had sewn bright red corduroy patches on the knees for Daniel.

When he came home from school the day he wore them, he said that the high school girl who was helping with the kindergartners had mocked his patches. "But," he said gently, "she doesn't know Jesus, so she can't help it." I was amazed at his understanding of what a change Christ makes in a life, and how that understanding shielded him from really being hurt. I was so deeply grateful!

I have heard or read how some would take time spent waiting: for a light to change, someone to answer the phone or come to the door, etc. to just tell the Lord, "I love you, God. I really love you, Lord. You are so precious to me, Father." This can be done anytime—while dishwashing, car washing, showering, jogging, carrying out the trash, etc.—and the Lord used one of our sons to show me by a small "happening" that spontaneity of love could bring joy to His heart.

Our children loved to play outside. The boys would scrape little roads into the dirt of the driveway, and little trucks, cars, and tractors would buzz along them for hours. And this reminds me of an idea that bears mentioning. Instead of saying, "Go play," it would be so beneficial to take five minutes and set up a "play plan." "Honey—this rock could be a gas station, and these sticks the gas pumps, with the dandelion stems the hoses," etc. Or, "this rock could be a stove, these leaves dishes," etc. It will set their little minds into busy activity. This keeps them from getting bored and keeps them playing happily. Also, it is very important to be alert to attitudes—selfishness, sharing, and kindness, and deal with them as warranted. By the way, compliments for good behavior are like fertilizer. They make the good stuff grow!

But back to the boys. Understandably, when your truck has to haul fifteen loads of pebbles to your brothers' building site, all else gets put on the bottom of the list of important things to do. However, there is one thing that cannot and will not be ignored.

One morning, I was at the kitchen sink busily doing breakfast dishes. (Now remember, at the left end of the sink counter was the door to that most important room—the bathroom.) Suddenly David—then about four-and-a-half years old, burst into the kitchen and ran toward the bathroom. As he passed me, he grabbed me around the legs, buckling my knees, and kissed the back of my skirt. "Love you, Mommy!" he yelled and tore into the bathroom. My heart just leapt! That brought me such joy! I have thought of it often, even though David is an adult now. "See ya!" he yelled as he dashed out.

Goodnight and good-bye kisses, given dutifully on request are nice, and I'll take a hug anytime. But spontaneous love expressions are wonderful! Does not the Father-heart of our wonderful God feel the same and more?

May we not be time-wasters—but use our time to build a warm, close relationship with God. Begin, as my husband and I did and the Scriptures tell us we must, in John's Gospel, chapter 3 by giving the Lord your heart—the seat of your affections and life, and ask Him to forgive your sins and be Lord, King, Ruler over you. Then, of course, read the Bible daily. The Gospel of John is a good place to start. Attend a church that preaches from the Bible and believes it, and in your daily life be diligent to build a relationship with God: close, warm and loving. You will find peace, and a sense of fulfillment that nothing—absolutely nothing—can duplicate.

One little thing happened that was a rather startling eye opener to me. It had to do with the "Judge not, that ye be not judged" (Matt. 7:1–2) and Romans 2:1, where it speaks of the "judger" doing the same things.

The fashion world had just introduced the miniskirt. One of the young college students wore one, and the wife of one of the professors, a very sweet and gentle young woman, made a remark about it to the rest of us ladies. Amazingly, though, in about a week or so, that very same professor's wife had a miniskirt of her own!

That really put a caution on my life! Certainly I've slipped at times, but the Lord kindly and very quickly lets me know He wasn't pleased with what I have said or thought about an individual. I try to remember the Lord loves them or to pray He would touch them. It really did shake me good.

The Bible study group began to meet Sundays in the chapel, and one Sunday, another gentleman joined us. That evening service I shared a thought. The children had a plastic cross that glowed in the dark, and I had told them that the cross only glowed after it had been near light. It reminds us that we can only shine for Jesus (i.e., act like Him and show His love to others) if we get close to Him. We need time to be recharged by reading our Bibles and prayer, so we can be a blessing. It was just "something from a Mommy's heart"—no big pronouncement.

However, the other gentleman was of a persuasion that believed women should be "seen and not heard," and spoke to the professors, convincing them this was the way things should be done. Also, it was explained that having a pastor was not the right direction, but each man should be ready to give a message.

The Bible says in Romans 8:28, "And we know that all things work together for good to them who love God, who are called according to His purpose."

I am a first-born—with the tendency to be a leader. But the Bible clearly says that the husband is to be the head of the home (1 Cor. 11:3 and Eph. 5:23), not as a dictator but as a leader.

Don is a second-born and not a leader by nature. The Lord put us into this situation to mellow me down. It was very necessary, but thankfully another trait of a first-born is the desire to please—so I really tried to be submissive, and obey the Lord.

Now there is a big difference in being in submission, and under subjection. A wife is to be a help to her husband—a team member. Things need to be discussed, and she certainly should share her perception of the matter. But when the final decision is made, the husband is the one to do it. Hopefully, the decision comes after the couple has prayed together for God's leading.

The group, however, seemed to teach subjection rather than godly submission—i.e., the wife just follows without much input. But as I said, the Lord works all things together for good, and He used this time to do a good work in me, for which I'm truly grateful.

A little aside—one time the gentleman stopped by for a few moments to visit. Something I said to him wasn't completely the truth, and after he left, it bothered me.

In a short time, our Laura was lying on the couch with a terrible headache and asked her daddy to pray for her.

Right away I remembered the half-truth, so I told Don I had to go. (He probably thought I was going for aspirin or the like.)

I went right to the gentleman's house and fessed up. He very graciously pointed out a verse in Proverbs 27:19, which reads, "As in water face answereth to face, so the heart of man to man." In other words, we all have similar weaknesses.

I was there just a few minutes, then scooted back home. When I walked in, Don said, "I prayed, and Laura said, 'Daddy, it's gone!'" God is so kind.

May He help us all to humble ourselves and be transparent to one another.

At the Fair

I had been teaching classes with the elderly pastor at the Baptist church and had been receiving a magazine from Child Evangelism as a resource. In one of the issues was an article with outreach ideas. One suggestion was to have a booth at the county fair. It seemed like a good idea, so I prayed, "Lord, if You want us to do this, please have Don say 'Yes,'" and I went into the living room to ask him.

He said, "Yes."

The booth would be lined with large Bible story teaching cards (about sixteen by fourteen inches) of David and Goliath and the Prodigal Son, and I would tell stories to children and give out tracts. It was a very wonderful experience. The children and I camped in a tent, and were allowed to use the shower facilities provided for the folks that ran and exhibited at the fair. I was able to have some great conversations with some of the vendors and carnival workers.

The second year we were there, a "biker" person who had come onto the campus during the camp meeting at the Bible school hitch-hiked to join us! That particular camp meeting had ended up being rather wild! A group of about five bikers came on campus to get away from some others that were chasing and shooting at them. They were befriended by various camper families, taken to the service, and then tucked into various family groups for the night. Don came up to the camp meeting, and we got a young man and tucked him into the boys' tent with Don. In the morning he was sober and really receptive to the Lord.

Wonderfully, many of the young men that had come on campus surrendered their lives to Christ. Our young man so sincerely wanted to do something for God that he stood with me on the last evening at the fair giving out tracts. He had hitchhiked to our home to see us, and Don had brought him up to the fair. The Lord is *so* good!

9

Fun Here, There, and Everywhere

DON'S WORK AS an independent carpenter just wasn't able to provide for our family. He worked long hours, and often didn't charge for that last half hour, or the trip to get materials, and so on. So a dear friend we met in the church began to pray he would get other employment. That fall he entered the company he has since retired from.

In January or February of that winter, friends of ours invited us to come over and have dinner with them, and toward the end of the evening said yes, the momma dog's puppies were of the right age to be adopted out. Well, my husband absolutely is not a hard-hearted man, and with five eager children, and one cute, cuddly puppy we soon welcomed a new four-legged member to our family. We named her Tippy Tail Burns, as she had a white tip on her black tail, and two little white front feet, and a little white on her face. Otherwise, she was coal black, fat, playful and adored.

The next day, Sunday, we went to church and put Tippy (for short) on the enclosed porch. Someone may not have closed the door all the way, and poor Tip wriggled out into the snowy yard. When she tried to get back into the house through a cellar window, her little paw got caught in the screen and she was trapped to shiver in the snow until we got home. Don rescued her, and carried her into the house, putting her in a chair placed next to the kerosene stove which, with our landlord's help, we had purchased. She snuggled up to it, and began to lick it like it was her mother. That became her favorite spot, as long as we had that heater. She also became devoted to Don, and he allowed her to sleep at the end of our bed. That added a few "extras." (Fun to remember!)

Once we had friends come to stay overnight. We gave the couple our bedroom and bunked their children in with ours. In the dark, Tip took her usual spot at the foot of the bed. During the middle of the night, she woke up, apparently realized her "daddy" was not there, walked up our friend's chest and began to snarl in his face! Naturally, he bolted upright and said, "Tippy, remember me?"

When Don went on third shift, Tip was absolutely blown away by the weekends. During the week, she slept from eight or so in the morning with Don, until a little after four when he awoke. Then at night, she'd sleep at the foot of the bed with me, from about eleven o'clock or so until around six o'clock in the morning. Obviously she was well rested, averaging fifteen hours of sleep out of every twenty-four. When Don didn't go to bed Saturday or Sunday during the day—she just couldn't understand it. One night she kept giving him dirty looks, and finally gave up in disgust and just dragged her weary body off to the bed. It really was funny!

Tip also blessed us with five puppies, and of course our five children each had a favorite. I remember once coming into the house from hanging laundry and as I opened the screen door, five little furry bodies rushed past me to romp in the living room—followed by five blond-headed bodies, each whooping and chasing to get "their" puppy. It was a busy scene! Needless to say, we did find a good home for each puppy, and Tippy settled down to be the star of the show once more.

That little dog was a real joy to all of us. She really was cute, and one day we saw her trotting up the driveway, head held high, with one of the burned pancakes I had thrown out after breakfast in her mouth. She was on her way to bury it for later!

When Don was working nights for a while, Tippy was coaxed to sleep with the boys. Only she wouldn't sleep on top of the covers. Whichever boy whose turn it was to have her would hold up the covers, and she would burrow down to the bottom! The rooms were quite cold, and I could understand how much they enjoyed their "foot warmer."

Right around that time, the Lord blessed us with our sixth child—our fourth son, Douglas Steven. Perhaps because I had had three miscarriages, I was anxious and a bit fearful that this baby might not be whole. God was indeed again merciful, and the baby was whole. In fact, this may sound a little strange—but when the baby and I came home, the children joyfully showed me that I was not the only "Mommy" in the house. Our cat had had kittens in the boy's pajama drawer! And one of those kittens was born with only three good legs. We called it Blessing—because it seemed to me God was saying that something evil that might have been intended for us was interrupted by His merciful hand.

The baby was a dear, dimple-chinned, sturdy little fellow, with a sunny disposition. When he began to talk, his first phrase was "Bible—Jesus' Book," when he picked up the little New Testament at the end of our bed. My heart was thrilled! As he got older, Doug used to love to look out the window and "moo" at the landlord's cattle. Naturally, he picked up the nickname "Moo-Cow." He was Donny Jr.'s bunk buddy, and Donny designed a little cartoon "Moo-Cow" which we painted on the back of Doug's little jean jacket (which he still has). Once when we were on vacation, he wore it at an amusement park, and one of the biker-type attendants got quite a kick out of the little fellow's "colors."

Another thing I remember was when Doug was sitting on a little stool in the living room putting on his little play shorts to go outside. He looked at me so excitedly and said, "Look! They made a hole for the other leg too!" The things the children have said are all part of the weaving of precious memories that often still bring a happy chuckle.

One time when I was sweeping the back porch, Linda, at that time around four years old, called to me and said, "Mom, they're playing a song we sing at church on the radio! 'My Ankle's Cold.'" As you could guess, the song was "My Anchor Holds."

While Doug was still a babe-in-arms the Lord brought a very interesting gentleman into our lives, who has been a good and dear friend ever since. When Don worked as a carpenter, a young teenage boy used to watch and talk with him. He became a friend to our boys. On sunny days he bicycled out to see us and brought Dr. Paul Kohler, a remarkable language professor, with him. The children to this day call him Uncle Paul.

Whenever we could, we used to go on vacations. In the beginning, our plan was just to go somewhere and camp. When we were still living in Poughkeepsie, we packed a borrowed tent and gathered all our gear, along with our three children, ages one and a half, two and three-quarters and four and one-quarter years old. We headed out toward

Cape Cod and enjoyed the historic sights in our little VW Bug. Don made a bed like a platform on the back seat and we loaded the gear under it and on top. We took the little ones on the "Mayflower." Don had to carry our two and three-quarter-year-old daughter because she was absolutely sure she would fall through the cracks in the boardwalk.

The most memorable part of that trip for me was breaking camp. The tent had an umbrella-type pole structure with poles inside that snapped up and down like ribs of an umbrella. Well, Daddy was inside emptying the tent, figuring out how to unsnap the pole situation, when his three little friends decided to "help."

Quick as a wink, those little ones ran around the tent and pulled up all the stakes. Needless to say, the tent started teetering and rocking back and forth, and someone inside (I won't give a name) started hollering, "What's going ON?" Helpfully, all I could do was laugh till I could barely stand. That man has put up with a lot!

When we moved back to Poughkeepsie from the college the first time, a friend contacted a church there and asked the pastor to call on us. He did. But on the evening he chose, Don was fixing our wringer-washer on the back porch, and its motor had just slipped and dumped oil all over! The porch and Don were an absolute drippy mess, but since I was out "Avon-ing," he had to answer the front door. "Hello, Pastor."

Apparently Pastor Hayes wasn't scared by Don's slick appearance, and set up times to come and teach us from the Bible. (His was the church that so kindly remembered us when we went back to college.) One of the times he came, we had something "wild and woolly" (quite tame by today's fare, for sure) on the small black-and-white TV. Pastor didn't say much, but whatever it was made us realize that for us, TV watching was not a good choice.

So even though there was a set left over in the Red House when we moved in, it was put in the garage until the landlord could take it away.

What effect did that have on the children? Our oldest son was about twelve when the art teacher asked the class, "Who does not have TV?" Donny told us he hesitantly raised his hand to find he was the only one. But then the art teacher said, "I thought so, for you are more creative."

Not too long after that he gave us an example of that creativity. Don had gotten on the day shift, but, since he was working hard, found it difficult to get up in the morning. Without our knowing it, Donny Jr. decided to hook up an invention to help his Dad get up.

The boy took an old "oogah" horn from the old truck we had, and put it under our bed. Then he put snap clothespins on the blade of a small electric fan, and put it into my canner, laid on its side. He hooked it all up to the timer Don had gotten to turn the lights on in the chicken coop (just in case one of the hens possibly might figure out they could lay an egg!) He put it all onto a long extension cord, which he covered with our little scatter rug so we wouldn't notice it and plugged the other end out in the living room. After we went to bed, he crept onto the sofa to watch the action.

Because the bedroom was so small, Don's side of the bed was against the wall. There was a narrow aisle on my side and a little bit of room at the bottom of the bed. About six thirty in the morning, all of a sudden under our bed there was a loud OOGAH! OOGAH! OOGAH! DING! DING! DING!, DING! (clothespins hitting the canner sides).

Don literally *sprang* out of bed—didn't crawl over me at all. His eyes were as big as saucers as he crouched beside the bed trying to figure out what on *Earth* hit! Finally he found the cord, followed, and unplugged it. And do you know, Donny Jr. slept through all of it? He was a bit disgusted to have missed the action. Later, he made a very detailed drawing of a system to eject skunks from our friend's trash-cans. So much for the effects of no TV!

10

God's Mercy With the Nail

REMEMBER THE BIBLE study that began when we lived in Saxon Heights (the married student housing)? Well, we had been meeting together for quite some time and decided to use the little chapel, which became available, and have church there together. We all really enjoyed it, especially singing hymns together, and the men—especially a professor who had been a stevedore—would bring a message. We were considering calling a pastor.

It was a mixed group—college students, two professors, an elderly couple (in-laws of the stevedore), Don and I, and of course, everyone's children. We were good friends—like a family—and one summer we ladies decided to have a rummage sale to donate money to World Vision. The only thing was, we decided to have it at our house, four miles to a town in either direction on a *dirt* road! In other words, we had a rummage sale in the middle of nowhere! It was great fun, though, and we laughed a lot! We were sitting on the front porch step, taking a tea break, when I said, "Listen! Hear that?"

"No, what?"

"The sound of the chartered bus coming to our sale!" The girls couldn't believe I said that! It was great!

Earlier that morning, though, I had gotten wood together for the kitchen stove, so I could cook the children's oatmeal. To get pieces to fit the stove, it was necessary for me to cut them, as Don had not had time to do so. Now, there are pictures of "women of the hills" with a small ax cutting kindling, holding the piece of wood on a stump in their other hand.

Well, there was no way in the world I dared to do that, and my instrument of cutting, or rather bashing, was a great big ax on a big long handle. I would set a piece of wood in place, step forward, and bring the ax down with a good crack, wood splintering as it "would." (Pardon the pun.)

The only thing was that one of my steps forward was onto a nail, and I heard the "pop" as it pierced my tennis shoe and went into my foot. I pulled the nail out, and because of the time crunch went on with the necessary activities.

By evening, my foot was quite painful, and I began to see a red streak starting up my leg. We called the old family doctor, Dr. Hitchcock, and told him the problem. He said that if I soaked the foot in an Epsom salt solution and took it out of the water, the hole would seal up again. He said to wet a towel in solution as hot as I could stand, wrap my foot, and put it in a plastic bag. He said the "wet dressing" would allow the wound to continue to drain.

By bedtime, the foot was so painful I couldn't stand anything to touch it, so I didn't dare sleep in the bed with Don, in case he would roll over and bump it or cause the blankets to rub against it. The foot really hurt, so at my insistence, I spent a restless night on the living room floor. As I lay there unable to sleep, with my foot throbbing, I said

"Lord! Those nails must have hurt You *so much*!" Here I was with my wound comforted by the warm wet cloth, but He had no comfort and much, much greater pain. I was deeply moved.

When morning came, the streak was gone and so was the pain! What a blessing! Later when a finger wound became infected, I applied the same method of a "wet dressing," and it proved effective once again.

We enjoyed the college students, and they would sometimes come out to see us. One winter Saturday, a young man from New York City came just as I was firing up the wood kitchen stove so I could start cooking oatmeal for the family. He told us later that he couldn't imagine why I was putting paper under the big white coffee pot!

After church that Easter the same young man came to dinner. First, though, we had the awaited Easter egg hunt. The young man was very touched by the attitudes of the children, for the older ones were saying to the younger, "Look up in the light!" or "Look by the piano!"—helping their little friends to find the hidden treasures. He said he had not seen that kind of caring in a family, and I am so deeply grateful it is still there. Things like that are priceless beyond words.

The Lord Keeps His Hands on Us

The winter was a very heavy one, with lots of snow. The children really enjoyed playing in it, and I kept a box of mittens and hats out on the porch, with wet ones drying on the shelf of the kitchen stove all the time.

A little aside—Psalm 144 says that the Lord "teacheth my hands to war, and my fingers to fight" (v. 1). When I first read that I thought, "A fine surgeon!" But later I realized, He taught a little homemaker out on a dirt road how to stretch leftovers: (one small piece of meat, diced and boiled with bullion in an iron pot, makes the base for a vegetable soup for the next night's supper with of course homemade biscuits or corn bread.)

Also, He showed me that a shrunken sweater makes wonderfully warm mittens. The cuffs of the sleeves make the cuffs of the mittens, with the thumb part along the seam, and the finger-part the main body of the sleeve. Whip-stitch the cut part tightly, and you have snug, warm, no cost mittens! The body of the sweater can be made into tube socks and the shoulders into little slippers, also. They have been a real blessing!

Oatmeal was our breakfast. We bought it in fifty-pound bags from a health food store and it was much cheaper and quite tasty. I have since learned that oatmeal helps a child's learning! Amazing!

One Saturday morning I was boiling oatmeal for breakfast on the wood stove, and our son, Dale, just about two, was standing on a chair watching. Probably during a fun chase, our son, Doug, age three and a quarter, came running by and accidentally kicked the leg of the chair Dale was standing on. Dale had been holding on to the back of the chair and the blow sent it against the face of the stove top, pressing his little hand onto the hot metal. He cried out, and of course, I grabbed him away!

At that time, we had no phone, were out of bandages, and we were snowed in. I sent one of the children out to get some snow to put on his hand, then Don and I went into the bathroom to pray. With tears running down our faces, we asked the Lord to touch our baby. He stopped crying immediately!

I fixed him a bottle, and laid him down. When he got up, he came showing me the large blisters all across the base of the fingers of his right hand, calling them "funny bubbles"—but with no pain. Later, when playing in the living room with the children, the "bubbles" broke. He just walked into the kitchen, opened the cabinet door, took out one of our cheap (and stiff) paper napkins, blotted the water and went back to play. No pain. Later, all the "gang" wanted to go out and play in the snow—so with mittens on, out he went too. No pain, and no infection.

Many years later, in 1988, I blew up the oven in my face, badly burning my right hand. (We had moved, and had a large restaurant-style gas stove.) Three things showed me how kind the Lord was to me. First, though I saw the blue flames and had burns on my face, my eyes were unhurt. Second, when the emergency room doctor asked me if I had a cough, my answer was "No, but sir, why the question?" He explained that many people draw in breath at a shocking situation which causes the lungs to be burned. My reaction—when the car skids or something startling happens—is to call out "Jesus!", which I had done. His Wonderful Name truly is a shield.

Now, third, when I went to get the bandage changed two days later, the doctor asked if I had insurance. He said I'd better activate it, because I had cooked all the tendons in my hand and was looking at three months of therapy and possible surgery. Again the Lord's mercy was made manifest; that was spoken on a Wednesday, yet by Friday I didn't need bandages, and by Monday—one week after the accident—he dismissed me damage free. The Lord also prevented my face from having any scars and I found out later that that was a prayer of one of my friends.

The reason I brought up my little adventure here was to show again the Lord's kindness. Obviously, the tendons in a tiny little hand, "pressure cooked" by being pushed against the heat suffered a great deal more damage. But our Dale has never had one bit of impairment even as a little child.

However, as if to verify this story, Dale has a large scar all across the base of the fingers of his right hand. But, as I said, he never has had any impairment even from a young age, and as an adult, is very proficient on the computer, and plays the piano and keyboard. God is good!

A little aside—the hospital put pads of medicated gauze on my face, and to hold them in place, put a white plastic net bag over my head—something like what oranges are sold in, only white. They cut eye, nose, and mouth openings, and a tuft of hair was sticking out of the top, I later saw.

Our son who had taken me in to the hospital and was bringing me home teasingly said, "Mom, you can't go into the drugstore to pick up your prescription. They'll think you plan to rob the place!"

When our pastor came to visit and wanted a picture, I told him it would be the first camera on the moon! I really was a ridiculous sight. But stuff like that is fun to laugh at.

One thing that amazed me, as our son David, on orders from his father, was taking me to the emergency room in his truck ("Mom will you come or shall I carry you?" he had asked), the Lord gave me the song "Be Still My Soul" which I began to sing. It surprised both of us, but the words were so beautifully applicable.

> Be still my soul; the Lord is on thy side.
> Bear patiently the cross of grief or pain;
> Leave to thy God to order and provide.
> In every change, He faithful will remain.
> Be still my soul; thy best, thy Heav'nly Friend.

Through thorny ways leads to a joyful end.
Be still my soul, thy God doth undertake.
To guide the future as He has the past.
Thy hope, thy confidence let nothing shake.
All now mysterious shall be bright at last.
Be still my soul; the waves and winds still know.
His Voice Who ruled them when He dwelt below.
—"Be Still My Soul" by Katharina Von Schlegal,
Jane L. Borthwick, and Jean Sibelius

11

Adventures With the Holy Spirit

PERHAPS IN ANSWER to my heart's hunger, a friend of Don's began to pray for us in agreement with a minister that we would enter into another step in our relationship with Jesus Christ.

My gift to the family for Christmas was a spotlessly clean house. The process started after all the children were tucked in, winding up with my stuffing a turkey and putting it in the oven. Then I would sit on a chair in the kitchen to keep the fire going and doze a little.

Our youngest daughter said she would lay awake listening to the old mantle clock Don's folks had passed on to us chime the hours. When six o'clock rang, (the hour of wake up!) the house burst into life!

Our Christmas mornings were never a dive-in frenzy. Don read Luke 2:1–14, then we prayed and gave out the gifts! We still do that, and it is such a priceless joy to me to have our dear family all gather in our home to continue with that tradition. Now there is quite a bunch! Would you believe we number forty-three? God is so good! I am grateful beyond words!

After all the day's activities—dinner, clean up, etc—I was a bit tired. Not long after the children were tucked in, the friend who had been praying for us showed up. He sat at the end of our kitchen table, and began to share scriptures with Don about being filled with the Holy Spirit, and receiving a prayer language, as in Acts 2 and 1 Corinthians 12:4–10.

The group we had been a part of—the ones who didn't believe women should speak in church (Don says they *were* allowed to breathe!)—were also very strong on teachings about the historical Jesus, the Christian life, and deeply revered the Scriptures. However, the dear ones were not much on prayer or power in prayer.

When Don's friend began to share scriptures with him, I was sitting across the table from him and, to be honest, fighting to keep awake. But with each scripture spoken, Don looked as if his face was being slapped—though the words were not spoken at all harshly.

After the friend finished sharing, he asked Don if he would like to be filled with the Holy Spirit. Don roused me, and together we went and knelt by the couch in the living room, where we were prayed for. The Lord graciously filled us with His Holy Spirit, and we both received our prayer language.

So what happened? For one, it showed me there *was* more, answering a cry of my heart!

Praying in tongues in the prayer language given by the Holy Spirit can be a language of men and of angels. (See Acts 2:4 and 1 Corinthians 13:1.)

But we also speak mysteries to God and edify—strengthen and build up spiritually—ourselves (1 Cor. 14:2–4).

Don't forget, the stronger we are spiritually, the more we can be used by the Lord, which can be very gratifying—and fun and exciting too!

When we pray in our prayer language, our heartfelt joys, gratitude, and love for God, or our deepest anguish—all beyond our ability to articulate—can be expressed.

There are many incidents throughout my life that can illustrate this.

The first was as a bride-matron in my sister's wedding. As I got ready and then walked down the aisle, I prayed quietly in tongues, imperceptible to those around me. The Lord gave me such a sweet peace. And later, I heard someone had commented that I looked so peaceful. To God be the glory.

The second incident is a bit more dramatic.

When our youngest child, Darin, was about a year and a half or two, we babysat a little boy, B. T., about three years old who lived across the road from us. We had, before the birth of Darin, moved down into the little town.

One afternoon, the little guys were sitting on our oldest son's big yellow motorcycle that was "parked" on our little front porch. They were busy "riding" it, so I took the minute to run upstairs. As I was tidying my hair—no longer than three or four minutes from when I left the boys—to my horror, I looked out the bathroom window to see B. T. running up the road beside our house, heading toward the highway with our little one trailing behind.

I raced down steps, out the backdoor of the house, and sprinted as fast as I could go up the road. When I called to him, he looked back at me with a big grin as if we were playing a game and darted across the highway—right into the path of a car coming from town.

The car's brakes squealed, but there was a dull thud and I watched as the little guy flew up in the air and came down into the asphalt.

I kept right on running.

The Lord must have sent an angel, for Darin didn't follow me. Immediately I knelt in the road beside the still little form, laid my hands on him, and began to pray in tongues for him from the depth of my being.

The young man who was driving the car jumped out and said, "Oh, I'm so glad to hear you praying!" The trooper came, the ambulance came, and a neighbor took me to the emergency room. (By the way, the trooper said the measurements showed the young man was going the thirty miles per hour speed limit.)

The ER staff was busy working over B. T., and of course, I was not allowed near. In the corner of the adjoining room, I knelt over his little coat that had been cast aside, my head nearly on my knees, prayed in my prayer language again, from the very depth of my being until a nurse came and asked, "Are you all right?"

The agony inside can hardly be described. It's terrible enough when the injured child is yours, but when it is one you were entrusted to care for? It is times like this (which I wouldn't wish on anyone!) that being able to have a way to put into words one's intense emotions is such an priceless, immeasurable blessing.

The little one was sent up to Strong Memorial in Rochester, and of course, many in our little community held him up in prayer.

The accident happened on a Wednesday, and to our joyful amazement, on Saturday he came home!

A few weeks after, our daughter Linda injured her leg while playing in a barn at a home were we were having a "singspiration." This is a prime example of God working "all things together for good" (Rom. 8:28). It was x-rayed and put into a cast—but it became so uncomfortable I took her to the doctor's in just a few days. Another X-ray was taken, and the cast removed, for there was no break. (Prayer answered?)

Our son Darin and B. T. were with me, and I asked the doctor—who happened to be the one on duty in the ER when B. T. was hit—if he remembered him. "Oh yes!" he said, ruffling B. T.'s hair. "I was *so* concerned when I sent him to Strong! He not only had blood coming from his ear—but brain fluid!" B. T. is now a strong, capable, adult, absolutely fine. God is so very kind. I am deeply, deeply grateful. I guess the conclusion to this little "adventure segment" is:

1. If you have not asked Jesus to be your Lord and Savior, do so.

2. Then, ask Him to fill you with His Holy Spirit and grant you the gift of tongues. He wants to do that.

Repercussions From God's Touch

We were a little hesitant to spill the beans to the little group about what had happened to us, as they were pretty much against it. Usually I was the one to go to the Bible study with the admonition, "Don't say anything" (about our experience of receiving our prayer languages).

This went on for a while, but one evening, one of the college students had asked, "Now that I've been saved, what's next?" The answer was to keep reading his Bible, and living as it said, go to church, and pray. The dear ones at the Bible study found it difficult to pray for any length of time at all, and even said as much. But as I have said, they dearly loved the Scriptures and the Lord. Perhaps they were afraid of things that may be out of the ordinary, spiritually speaking.

Anyway, I came home from the Bible study that evening ready to burst and told Don I had to be able to say something! Well, that Sunday Don shared in the little chapel service about how the Lord had been moving on the island of Timor. Apparently a missionary had told the people that the big rock they held to be a god was not one at all, and as he challenged it, the rock split in half in front of them. Don had read about this in the magazine put out by the denomination of the little church we had been attending before.

The following week—perhaps Tuesday or Wednesday—three men from the church, the leadership, came out to the little red house to tell us they did not want us to come to the chapel, the Bible study, or in any way fellowship with any of them again, including our children with theirs.

I was absolutely devastated and after they left knelt by our sofa and *cried*! I was so very sorry the gang that we loved so much was not willing to receive more from the Lord, and I was also so very sorry for our children, for they were absolutely best friends with the gang's children!

But our darling family never said one word of rebuke to us about the situation! Not even a murmur. That was so very *kind* of them! It was strange, though. That very morning when I was ducking under the fence after feeding the landlord's animals, the song "This Is My Valley" came very strongly to me. I was a bit surprised, and wondered what it might mean. I felt it was the Lord preparing me for something, and that evening I understood it.

We had met a couple in a small town nearby through a friend and fellowshiped with them, and even went to their home town in Pennsylvania to some special meetings. We also heard of the Full Gospel Business Men's Fellowship, and went to their meetings in a town nearby. It was a blessing to hear men tell of their spiritual journey as they found their way to life in Christ, and what adventures He had them on.

In our living room, we began to have meetings also. The Lord even used one of those meetings to encourage a pastor who was absolutely ready to quit the pastorate, to continue. We are so very grateful, and today he not only has a wonderful church, but many, if not all of his family, are in ministry, some by music! One time we even were able to have the privilege of the Cameron family from Scotland holding a concert in our dining room! There were about forty people or more that came to hear them, and Don and Joe were concerned about the floor beams, especially when the folks began to stomp a bit to the music!

We also learned about a Bible school that had a camp meeting, where one could tent at very low cost on the sports field. Don didn't have vacation at that time, so for several years he let me take the children, and any others I could gather, and go there to camp for a week. (This is the camp I mentioned earlier.)

We had two "oldish" tents, a boys' tent and a girls' tent—and often I had fourteen children with me. As I remember, Don would help set us up, then he and Donny (about fifteen years old) would head back home. One thing rather amusing about that. Don really likes spaghetti—and one time he cooked a full heaping three pounds for the two of them! They did have enough.

The camp meeting was always wonderful, with a lot of beautiful worship and praise music. I remember coming back into the service after taking our little girl to the ladies room and feeling the presence of the Lord so strongly as a quartet was singing I was stopped in my tracks, literally unable to move. Wow!

There were special meetings for the children, and when I saw children of eight, nine, ten, etc., with their hands raised in worship, and even tears on their faces, it awakened a deep, deep longing in my heart that our children and the children I brought with me would love the Lord that sincerely too.

As far as the setup—I cooked on a camp stove, and we all slept on blankets or quilts on the tent floors and covered with more of the same. We also were allowed to use the college laundry-mat and ironing board, which, with the number of children with me, was a real blessing! I would take a big plastic bag or two full of dirty clothes and towels, etc., up the hill, while the children were in the afternoon activities. I met several missionary wives there, but I think my laundry quantity and frequency topped them all. But I was so sincerely grateful to be there, for I so wanted the children to be touched by the Lord.

After we had done this for several years, by the way, the president of the college happened to run into me. Apparently, he had heard of us, and asked me what I was sleeping on. When I told him, he said, "You are not sixteen anymore. Wait here and I will bring you a cot." I was so touched by his kindness—for I wasn't even one of his students.

Some of the children from town that went with us to the camp really became friends, and unbelievably, during the cold, blustery winters about five to seven of them would hike the four miles up over the hills to our house on Saturdays! They would just show up, and I would make them homemade hot cocoa and bake oatmeal cookies if we didn't have any on hand. I was truly amazed! Even now, I feel very privileged that they would do that.

Then, when we did move into town, they would all come and gather at our house for prayer before they left for school. In fact, the neighbor lady commented to another who told me that she had heard there was a big family moving in next to her, but was worried what she was in for when she counted *thirteen* children leaving for school!

Some of these children had met me—and thankfully, the Lord—at the afternoon religious instruction class held at the Baptist church. I began to help the elderly pastor and made a flannel board, and put the words of songs on large sheets of flexible white plastic which were fastened on a board by rings. We would then have a teaching story. (I had also done this with the "Chapel Gang" before.)

It was a real blessing, and I enjoyed it greatly. I would bring my "little friends" (our youngest children), as the pastor would come and get us every Thursday afternoon.

One winter afternoon on a day the wind had been blowing hard since morning, the pastor didn't come. One of the older children, I believe it was David, was home with a genuine, not faked, malady—perhaps a cold.

I really felt uneasy, so I asked him to watch over the little ones, while I walked into town to see if all was well. About three-quarters of a mile from the end of the road, I saw the dear elderly pastor stuck in a drifted snow bank. He was trying desperately to get out, but try as he might, the car was dug into the drift. I was so *very* glad I had come, and the Lord helped me to push enough so he could get free. When we got to the church, thankfully those helping us had kept the children singing and contented, so we could go right into the story-lesson.

12

Seven Plus Seven Equals Fourteen

ONE EVENING IN the early fall of 1970, Don answered the phone to hear the voice of a friend, in tears, saying, "My wife has left me." Joe had four small children and was at a loss as to what to do. I heard my husband say, "Why don't you come over and live with us?" And later that evening Joe and his little family—Sam, age five; Sally, four; Shirley, three; and Susie, one and a half—moved in.

About two weeks later our oldest son, Donny, came home from school and said, "Mom, there is a little girl on the bus crying. Her mother left them. Can she and her little brother come live with us too?" So, after contacting their father, it was agreed that Helen, age seven, and Henry, age four, would stay with us during the week and their daddy would have them on weekends.

A short time after that the county jail called to let us know that the sixteen-year-old we had said we would be glad to give a home to was "ready"—so Don and Joe went to bring Eugene to join the crowd.

When everything settled, our household looked like this:

- A sixteen-year-old—Eugene
- Our oldest son—Donny Jr., fourteen
- Our oldest daughter—Laura, almost thirteen
- Our next son—David, eleven and one-half
- Our next son—Daniel, nine
- Our next daughter—Linda, seven
- Helen, seven
- Sam, five
- Henry and Sally, four
- Our son—Douglas, and Shirley, three
- Our son—Dale, and Susie, one-and-a-half
- Two "Daddies"—my Don, and Joe
- One "Mommy"

And I cooked on a wood stove.

The children totaled fourteen, with nine of them ages seven and under, so it was a bit of a busy household, but it was fun. The Lord definitely was with us, and without His strength, help, and guidance, it would have been an impossible task. With Him as the center of our household, there was joy for the journey, and I can look back with a deep gratitude. He truly does equip us for what He calls us to, and we do not have to be a bit afraid.

Even if life might look scary, as our yard did to our little four-and-a-half-year old Daniel one darkening evening as he watched me from the top porch step head over to our car to go to prayer meeting, I have learned by all this, and you will find—to quote him—"Mommy, there's not really any bears out there!"

God Provides for Our Expansion

In the evenings, about seven o'clock, we would all gather in the living room for family devotions (the path the dear elderly lady had put us on years ago). The Lord put that time in our hearts because He knew the little ones would not be too tired. (He is so smart!)

We'd sit around—often with me on the floor, with several little people on my lap—and sing while my husband played the piano. We had several little wooden tambourines, and the children loved to take turns with them. My husband could always tell, however, when our oldest daughter played the tambourine, for even at her young age, she was very good. Don would share a little scripture with a little word of explanation. Then we'd all "pray around"—usually beginning with the youngest, until all had prayed.

As you can imagine our kitchen was a bit crowded, with the fourteen children and two Daddies at the table. I did sit too, but often was busy going around the table: "I'll get it, honey. Here's some butter for that. Don't put your fingers in there. Just a minute, I'll wipe that up"—and so forth.

Don asked our landlord about building on a dining room. The man agreed and said he would buy all the blocks and cement, but he wouldn't be able to provide the wood. That night, at family devotions, Don explained to the children what was being planned, and that we needed to ask the Lord to provide wood. The heavenly Father must have enjoyed hearing all the dear little ones praying, "Dear Jesus, please give us wood for our addition."

Not too long afterwards, while using a friend's truck to bring in the blocks, Don got a ticket for "air pollution." (Don said if it were any worse the man wouldn't have even seen him!) When he went to pay the five dollar fine, off the top of his head he asked the judge if by chance he knew of anyone tearing down a house, so he could buy some wood.

That judge replied, "There's a man tearing a house down, down the street. He is so sick of it, he'll probably *give* it to you!"

That is exactly what happened! The man had taken away all the lath and plaster and other "mess," so Don, Joe, and the older boys were able to easily get the absolutely adequate wood supply for free! We also were able to get windows from the student housing apartments we had lived in, which were all in the process of being torn down. God so provides!

Don built a sixteen-foot-by-twenty-foot addition, and our very first meal in it was Thanksgiving dinner. I neglected to mention that during this time Don and Joe had helped an elderly lady move, and she gave them a huge table which she didn't need—and we sure did!—so we even had a table for our new room.

We prayed about what wallpaper to use, and felt led to choose a colonial red with snowflake design—a bit similar to the living room. One night the room filled with smoke from a fire in the stovepipe of the wood stove in the room.

No damage was done, but the smoke, which didn't harm the red paper at all, would have ruined the other design we liked that had a white background. But we had prayed and felt led to use the red. And would you believe the red wallpaper's name was "King's Choice." We noticed that later.

Heartache

At the beginning of the second summer, Joe and his wife reconciled, rented a house, and were together as a family. We had switched things around and put the boys all in the larger bedroom and the girls where the boys had been. Not too long after that they came to visit and when it came time to go, our sons begged to have Sam stay overnight. Permission was granted—a little reluctantly on his mother's part—and everyone tucked in for the night.

The very next evening Joe called to say that while he was at work his wife had taken the girls and all the furniture and moved out. Don invited him to come. Sam was re-enrolled in school and things went along in usual fashion. Perhaps three weeks later, on a Saturday afternoon, Sam's mother came to get him. Sam had been very happy with us, enjoyed his "brothers," and was loved by them too.

When his mother Emily came, there was a lot of pleading on the children's part—some were near tears. Don and I were trying to reason with her also. Emily went into the bedroom where Sam's little dresser was to get his clothes, and the family all followed. Our son David laid down on the bunk bed Don had made, grabbed a post with one arm and Sam with the other, holding both as tight as he could. The memory of this still stirs up emotion in me.

Joe, too, explained it would not be good if she took Sam since he really didn't want to go. After a bit, she consented to leave without him, and we all breathed a sigh of relief.

One evening in the later part of January, Joe called Sam into the kitchen, where I was finishing the after-supper clean up.

"Get your coat. You're going to your mother's." That was all Joe said. I was stunned.

The little boy didn't say a word. He walked out on the shed porch, got his little leather jacket we had given him and with a glance in my direction walked out into the night. My heart felt like it was going to stop. Later, to hopefully make it easier for the boy, I washed, folded, and organized all the clothes he had left in his little dresser and sent that over to him. Apparently Emily was pleased with that.

I should say a little bit about Emily. As a child she had been moved about in several foster homes throughout the western U.S., apparently some not so good. She and Joe met while he was in the service. Don met Joe at Dresser-Rand, and we were introduced to Emily and infant Sam. When Joe decided to pursue a different vocation, we helped the family—by then with three children, and again when the household numbered six.

During that time I could see Emily struggled with self-worth. One time she showed me a little planter that was a gift from Joe—a combination Mother's Day and birthday present. She said, "Well, at least it is my favorite color, yellow." She, on the other hand, had saved quite a while to buy him a very nice gift and really seemed to try to please. When Don had gone with Joe to try to bring about reconciliation, she said to Don, "He doesn't love me."

My heart went out to her. Sometimes when we see an "event," it's easy to stand in judgment. Joe, too, was from a dysfunctional family, having been sent by his mother to live with his grandparents when he was about five years old. So though the situation was a difficult one, our hearts, knowing their backgrounds, went out to the both of them.

Eugene had been restless, and a bit difficult to get to cooperate in the family. He would leave, and we would pray with great concern. In a few hours we'd see him walking back down the road toward home. He had visitation rights with his mother. One time as I was taking him there and pouring my heart out to him about how greatly he needed to go God's way, he said, "Something is telling me she's lying."

He did return to his family not long after that, but his life, unfortunately, has been a rocky road. Our paths have crossed at various times, and he knows we care for him. He seems to care for us also. We pray for him and trust he will surrender to the One who loves him so very much. Helen and Henry also went back with their dad, who soon after married a very nice woman.

13

God's Helping Hand

WE WERE ALWAYS busy. At least I often found something to do, especially in the dishpan.

One Saturday when I was cleaning up after breakfast, one of the little ones came in for a drink of water. The "other daddy" happened to be standing by, and said, "Well, Irene, when you wash ninety-nine cups, one more doesn't make a difference." And that comment really did help to bring me peace when I felt a bit overloaded.

Not too far from us—perhaps three or four miles—was a small man-made lake, supported by the memberships of those who were then allowed to use it. By scraping and saving, between Joe and our family, we were able to come up with the thirty dollars necessary to become members.

Usually I didn't have a car. But one summer day, for a reason I can't remember, there was a vehicle in our yard. That day I had been baking. I usually made four or six times a recipe of oatmeal cookies, and then a batch of biscuits to get ready for supper. A store had turkeys on sale and I had gotten one to provide nourishing, inexpensive meat. When all the other baking was finished, and I had popped the turkey in the oven, the thermometer on the kitchen cabinet *across* the room from where I was working in front of the wood stove read 116 degrees Fahrenheit. (No kidding!)

The children had been told that if they all behaved, we'd go to the lake when the baking was finished, so everyone happily gathered to get into the station wagon when I called, except our oldest son. He had saved for quite a while—birthday gift money, and the little he could earn—to buy a small black motorcycle from the neighbor for twenty-five dollars. He asked if he could take it and a friend (Eugene's brother who was visiting) to the lake. I was happy to say yes, for he really enjoyed the bike.

A little aside that has meant a lot to me: Mrs. Billy Graham said that when we give permission to our child—to go outside, go play, snack, etc., we should do it with a "and have a good time" ring in our voice. If we say it with an "oh, all right you can"—with reluctance or irritation—it causes them shame and guilt, which robs them of the pleasure they could have had playing, visiting friends, etc. So I've tried, when I can say yes, to say it very soundly!

Well, our little gang had a wonderful time paddling around in the water. Finally, it came time to go home and get supper for the two daddies and check the turkey. When the boys decided to leave ahead of the family, there was no motorcycle key! That started the bustle of dumping out the dozen plus pairs of sneakers, shaking out towels, and feeling all around the area through the grass. Finally, when no key turned up, I said to the children, "Sweeties, we are going to have to pray."

We joined hands in a ring with almost all of the children and prayed, "Jesus, please help us find the key." Our son, Doug, about three, was playing at the waters edge in the mud, and honestly, as soon as that sentence was spoken, little

Doug came running over to us from the muddy shoreline. "Look what I found!" In his little hand was the motorcycle key—about the size of a child's thumb, and it had no "dilly-bob" attached! We were amazed, and literally jumped with joy. God is so good!

Because he was a little older, Donny could stay up just a while longer than the rest of the little gang. Of course, his evening activity involved the motorcycle. He really enjoyed riding around the yard. One evening while I was doing the dishes, Don heard a noise and went to check. He found that Donny had been driving his bike up to the window of the girls' bedroom, which was on the first floor, and our Linda and Helen would climb out and take turns getting rides. Don caught them climbing back in the window. Everyone was surprised that time!

One thing I've always been grateful for is that Don has never disciplined the children in a manner that made them afraid of him. Of the two of us, I probably would win the poll of who was the most strict.

The little house had a front porch, which I mentioned, and Don had enclosed it with windows someone gave him. It made an ideal playhouse for the girls and they all loved it, and filled it with dolls, dress-up clothes, and dishes.

When we were in between our times at college, Don had made a little wooden stove painted white, with dowels painted black and placed to represent four burners on top. It had an oven, and a little door on the bottom for the broiler. It was so cute, and of course, a hit with the girls. He also made a little hutch cabinet, with doors on the bottom, and wrought iron hinges and clasp from wood given to him on the construction sites he worked at in college. He also had made a car and picnic table while at college. Those two items are gone, though we have pictures, but we still have the stove and hutch.

Of course, the boys didn't want to let the girls enjoy their "house," so there was an occasional "rumpus." One cause for excitement was when her brothers put Sam in our daughter's little baby-doll buggy, and rammed down the road with him. Needless to say, the buggy didn't survive.

We used to get peanut butter from the Health Food Co-op in the equivalent of a tar pail—forty pounds at a time. It was the kind that had to be stirred to mix in the oil, but it was just ground peanuts. It was cheaper by far than commercial brands, and without additives, the children were getting the pure nourishment of the nuts. I often made my own bread, and more often biscuits. I tried to always buy jam instead of jelly, because more of the fruit was used to make it, and added extra powdered milk to both bread and biscuits, with sea salt, the salt of choice, and unbleached flour (much greater vitamin content). The Lord kept guiding me to boost the nutritious value of the food as much as possible, even with our limited budget. Just a little change of ingredients or additions can make a world of difference in the quality of the nourishment. And it pays off in good health. I also gave the children little iron tablets and chewable dolomite tablets.

As I have mentioned, across the driveway from the house, was a long four bay garage, very old, with the shed on the end. The boys decided the upstairs of the shed would be a "clubhouse." To bribe their sister, they had her make peanut butter and jelly sandwiches, put them in a little basket and wheel them out to the clubhouse on the pulley clothesline. Then the creeps wouldn't let her in! Yes, we were a normal family, with the typical rivalries.

One of those was over which was best—mayonnaise or salad dressing! And would you believe the children would be in two bunches, according to preference, and yell their favorite's name at each other? What some will do to pass the time!

Our David was a bit of an adventurer and one day decided to lead the "troops" across that long old garage roof and into the small trap door up on the attached shed. As they were going along, I probably had my hands in the dishpan, and didn't dream of such a venture! Suddenly, Helen fell through the roof—right into the center of a stack of old tires. What a mercy of the Lord! She was wedged in the tires, hands at her sides and never touched the ground, absolutely unhurt. I still am amazed at things like this. God is so kind!

I was concerned the children were not getting enough milk, so it was decided to get a milk goat. The children named her "Goatie," and she was quite a character. She greatly enjoyed flowers—plastic flowers—and one day I noticed her running across the yard with a plastic stick dangling from her mouth with a white flower pot on the end. That was all that was left of the plastic geranium the family had given me for Mother's Day!

She also got us in trouble by eating the landlady's cabbages, and one time even pushed her way into the house when a bunch of the gang was coming in. She must have smelled the oatmeal cookies which I had placed on paper on top of the washer and dryer to cool. She gave a yank, and a bunch of cookies hit the floor at her feet! Talk about commotion! Children yelling, me trying to keep her away from the cookies that were left, and everyone trying to budge her out the door. Whew! Now that's excitement!

She also pulled the same stunt a few days after Christmas and attacked the Christmas tree. We finally got her out the back door only to see her jump, stiff-legged in anger, to the front door and eat the plastic wreath hanging on it!

Another time she put her head into our plastic trash can with a swinging lid top. It caught on her head, and I looked out to see a bunch of children trying to catch Goatie as she ran with the lid around her neck like a collar. Never a dull moment! Goatie loved Don, and would chase after him if he happened to go to the garage to get a tool, with an "Oh, he left me!" look on her face.

As for the milk, even though Don was very careful to strain and chill it quickly, the only ones who would drink it were the "little people." One time I tried to disguise the taste and make homemade chocolate pudding with it, but was asked, "Mom, did you make this with goat's milk?" Of course, I had to admit it.

When I was a child, my mother was a stickler for the truth. One time—when I must have "told one"—she said, "I see L-I-E in your eyes!" I honestly could hear it ring up like the old-time cash registers used to clang $2.98 and turned to my sister to ask, "Can you see that in there?" It's funny now, but I was serious!

I felt the same way about my own family, and knew the thing I wanted to have them be able to trust in was my absolute honesty. I am so very grateful they do yet.

It is very demoralizing to a child to find out what you said was untrue. And as parents, we cannot expect the children in our care to be honest if they cannot trust our word. Having the children trust you is a priceless, priceless jewel, and it is not foolish to go back and say, "I was wrong, and I misled you here. Please forgive me." Humbling yourself to be honest will only increase your child's respect and confidence in you.

Goatie had a kid, named Billy—and the boys liked to play the game "Butt" with him, a head-to-head match. It wasn't long before that became a bit painful and was abandoned as an entertainment.

We also had chickens once again, perhaps about fifteen or so, who kept Goatie and Billy company in the bottom of the shed. These chickens also had absolutely no idea of their calling in life (eggs). But we would let them out, to at least keep the bug population down, which they were happy to do. But every once in a while the landlord or his wife would tell us to get the chickens back in the shed.

When that happened, the entire household—the two daddies and all the children—would run around the yard. Some of the older ones and the daddies had sticks, to put in the way of a chicken going north to make it turn west or east and hopefully be caught. It was a sight to watch and really funny!

One night as I was backing out of the driveway to go to prayer meeting, I was unable to drive for laughing. It was a hysterically, wonderful scene!

Another really funny thing also involved Goatie. At Don's folks' home during a visit, a TV advertisement was aired (and I don't remember the product) that showed a young man striding across a lovely field, with a beautiful Irish setter loping gracefully behind him.

Some time later, it was needful that we use the neighbor's phone, so Don and I trudged up the dusty road. Don, wearing a beat up hat, old clothes, and older rubber barn boots, scuffled his way up the hill. I glanced back to see Goatie, *great* with child, lumbering along to catch up to us.

Right away, the picture of the TV ad flashed into my mind. What a contrast! It really made me laugh!

14

Enjoying the Children

THERE WAS ALSO the natural "showing of special abilities" that makes an impression. Sally told me as an adult remembering our son Donny claiming he could drink a glass of water while he was upside down. She said she watched him do it and knowing Donny, I can believe it!

Donny Jr. also loved to tease. One April Fools' Day he switched the sugar bowl contents with that of the salt shaker. His Dad couldn't understand why the slice of tomato just wouldn't taste salted (sugar in the shaker just doesn't work), but when he stirred two spoon of sugar in his coffee and took a nice mouthful, he ran to the bathroom to get rid of it.

And one time, when Don was on his back under the kitchen sink fixing a leak, he called to Donny to get him a mirror so he could see up in a difficult place. That boy hurried up with an excited announcement: "Dad, I found this full-length pocket mirror!"

"Give it to me, Donny!" He handed his father a little plastic figure from a Noah's ark set the gas station had been giving away piece by piece. It was a three inch black gorilla!

There is something I want to be sure to mention about Donny. In 1965, Don had been able to purchase a bright red 1963 Ford Falcon station wagon. It was a real blessing, but our road was very hard on it, and it is the absolute truth that Don put in two engines and two "rear-ends" (you car people know what that is) to keep it going. It was cheaper than trying to buy another car.

I'm sure Donny was enlisted to help with those activities, but one project really touched my heart. The transmission also went bad and absolutely had to be replaced, for at that time the car was our only transportation. The only thing was, it was in the dead of winter. The old garage was full of wood and some of our landlord's things. That meant the old transmission had to be taken out and the new one installed—in the icy driveway.

Donny and his dad would work outside under the car, on their backs in the driveway as long as possible. Then they would come in and try to warm their hands by the wood stove. In a few minutes, out they would go again for as long as they could stand it. It was a brutal, painful job, but the boy stuck with his father until it was finished, even though the thermometer hovered at seventeen to nineteen degrees Fahrenheit.

Through the whole ordeal, Donny never complained or asked to be let off from helping. He was quite a boy, and that attitude (and his impressive capabilities) were such a blessing to his father—and to all of us!

I mentioned the landlady's cabbages. They were planted in a garden plowed up in the very back of our yard. When the garden was plowed, amazing rocks—half to two-thirds the size of a sofa cushion—were unearthed.

That gave me an inspiration. Every single morning, when the washer pumped out into the deep sink, I would get out my mop and race to mop the kitchen, bathroom, and dining room floors before all the water went down. (Of course, I had swept them first.) When you have fourteen pairs of young feet and three adults walking up a dirt path to come into the kitchen, things didn't stay clean-looking very long.

So I decided to take those rocks, which were at least six car lengths away, and move them into the path to the kitchen, to make a nice stone walkway. I tugged, pulled, hauled, and heaved, and—I did it! Success! A floor-saving stone path! Well, the next morning I awoke with very severe pain in my upper back and neck.

We had heard ministry about praying for the Lord to straighten back trouble, so I went into our bathroom and shut the door. As we had seen, I put my arms straight out at my sides, forming a *T*, then brought them together, palms lightly touching, and began to just thank the Lord.

My one arm began to jerk forward as if an unseen power was pulling it. Then it stopped and quickly the other arm began to do the same jerking movements. This went on for several minutes, then the movements stopped, and there were three releases of pain in my neck. I was absolutely amazed! Who was I that the Lord of the universe would bother with? I was so deeply grateful!

I also do want to mention, before going on, that I was so glad the landlady had her garden in our yard, even though Goatie caused a bit of difficulty with it. She was a very warm and pleasant person, and her garden gave us time to be together, which was quite enjoyable.

The winters were quite snowy and pretty cold. Beyond the garden was a small pond about two car lengths wide and long, and a little more than waist deep. Of course, the word was, "Do not go on the pond." But when there is an old bathtub nearby (the one that had been in our house), it just makes sense that it would be a fine ice raft—or something.

So of course, the boys got some long poles, pushed the tub onto, then naturally, through the ice, hopped in and began poling the tub around. All went well until the plug came out. Soon the kitchen porch was full of wet, cold, and rather sheepish-faced culprits—including some of the girls who had been on the ice at the time of the sinking. No one was hurt, and though I'm sure there was discipline for the disobedience, I couldn't help thinking it must have been fun and funny to watch!

God Is So Kind

I could have never done this without the Lord. But as we reach out to Him, He is more than there for us and will give us joy for the journey. One night, about 1:00 a.m., baby Susie was awake with a very high fever. As I walked the living room floor holding her in my arms, the verse came to my mind clearly, "And he stood over her, and rebuked the fever; and it left her" (Luke 4:39). (When Jesus healed Peter's mother-in-law.)

It came again, so I rebuked the fever in little Susie in the name of Jesus. It left her immediately. I put her back to bed and went to get some rest. One of our sons "pooh-poohed" the idea a little bit, and very soon had an earache. He then was glad to receive prayer and have the condition rebuked and leave.

Henry came down with what certainly appeared to be mumps. He was in bed, and in a good bit of pain. And again the Lord was so kind, as we prayed and rebuked the condition. He was just fine in about two days.

It was a busy time, but I look back on it with joy and gratitude for the privilege given to me. All the children we took in call us Dad and Mom or Uncle Don and Aunt Irene, and most of their children call us Grampa and Gramma, and we are so glad.

But I was particularly touched and surprised by Henry. Several years after he and Helen had returned home, Henry was working in a supermarket while in high school. I happened in, feeling a bit weary and looking, I'm sure, quite bedraggled. Suddenly I heard a strong, "Aunt Irene!" It was Henry, and he unashamedly gave me a hug right there! Later, when he was in college, he did the same thing! I was so touched that he cared more for me than for what others—even his peers who might see him—would think, and I treasure that memory. It's events like that that make things all worth while.

Many years later, hearing Sam introduce us to his Drill Sergeant when he graduated from Marine boot camp with "and this is my family" had the same impact. This memory too is a treasure to my heart.

15

Car Adventures

I WANT TO MENTION again that Don's heart was to provide the best for us. He has always felt badly that our cars were, at times, an "adventure." But to me, the adventures were funny! And we both would rather have the treasures of children than any luxury car ever available on Earth. (Besides, cars don't give hugs and smiles!)

Sometimes things are so funny when you look back on them. We had a light blue station wagon, and our oldest son Donny had begun doing fix-it projects on it. The main one was patching the two holes made in the hood by the motor mounts. Unfortunately, the patching compound was an ugly dark gray—rather conspicuous on the light blue hood.

My sister and her husband lived in Trenton, New Jersey, and invited us to bring the family for a visit. We were delighted, for it would give us a chance to show the children the Atlantic Ocean. A family we were friends with agreed to come housesit and take care of the chickens and Goatie. So we loaded our little bunch of eight children—plus Sam—into the "decorated" light blue Plymouth, and headed east.

The car, packed full of clothes and children, ran pretty well. When we stopped at a McDonald's (where the hamburgers used to be about twenty-five cents each), the clerk said he had never been given an order for nineteen burgers and nine milkshakes for a family and not a bus.

When we got to Trenton and settled in, plans were made for the boys to join my brother-in-law and his sons at a campsite just a little way from the home. Whether or not it happened as we went to the site, I don't remember, but the car developed a propensity to drop its muffler at the slightest provocation. It made any excursion a little interesting.

Our two nephews were not used to that type of car, so by the time we had made a few trips breaking camp, they were a bit unnerved by the sudden loud clang. The big day to go to the beach arrived, and my sister's boys wanted to ride along with the cousins.

The route to the shore led through a beautiful residential area of expensive homes. The car hit a little "whoops" in the road and the "clang" sat everyone rigid. Our oldest nephew's hands were white knuckled on the back of the driver's seat as he yelled, "It did it again!"

Don pulled the car up on a small bank in front of one of the beautiful homes that lined the street. Not only did the station wagon have a "decorated" hood, but the door behind the driver door didn't open. So when permission was given to exit, children began bailing out the side door, out the opened window of the door that didn't work, and out the opened window of the back. (Now don't forget, there were eleven—our eight, Sam, and our two nephews!) I got out of the front with the littlest one. It must have been quite a sight!

In no time at all, a patrol car pulled up. A concerned officer came up to Don, "Is anybody hurt?"

"No sir," my husband quipped, "I didn't have a wreck, I just drive one!"

While we're on the subject of our car adventures, here are a few more. As I had mentioned before, the house was nestled in a little valley on the dirt road, and the snow just blew across the road. The snow plows, and even at times a dozer, would come flying down the road to clear it.

In the process, time after time our little mailbox would be knocked off the post. Often we'd nestle it in the snow bank, only to have it knocked "akimbo."

So one summer, Don decided he'd *fix* the problem. He and the boys dug a hole, filled it with cement, and put in a piece of old barn beam. The mailbox was fixed firmly on top, and it was ready for winter (or so the guys thought!)

A few days later, we heard that a neighbor was sick. After supper, when the little ones were tucked in and the evening was settled, I got into our little red station wagon to visit them. I backed out, up the driveway, and square into the mailbox post, which broke completely off right at the ground!

Of course I stopped. I held my breath—but nothing happened! I had expected the house to empty, but no door opened. So, with my heart still pounding, I went up the road to the neighbors, and since Don had gone to bed before I left, when I got home, I quietly went to bed.

The next morning, there was something in the air as Don shaved, picked up his lunch, and left for work. My idea, however, was to fix him a great supper *then* fess up. (I hoped he would be so eager to get to work he wouldn't notice any of his surroundings on the way!)

Don left, and soon after, the children got up. "What happened, Mom? Why was Daddy so upset last night? He heard a noise, then got up and looked out the door. Then he started to yell, 'Nuts! Nuts! Nuts, nuts, NUTS!!'"

Then there was the time the little red station wagon wouldn't start. Don told me to get into it, and he would push it with the old truck. We started up the hill, and when I would pop the clutch at Don's instruction the car would make a terrible noise! Then I noticed I had it in reverse. I felt absolutely terrible. This was the *only* time I honestly felt I ought to pack and leave, for the only decent material thing on the earth Don had was the little red car, and here I was, ruining it.

Bless his heart, Don never rebuked me in a any way about my mistake, and I was so grateful that the car didn't seem any worse for wear. (Now, of course, I understand "things" are not what is most valuable in this life.)

Remember our icy driveway? Don felt a lot of pressure from his boss about being late for work, for often, even though he would leave the house early, by the time he got out of our driveway, he would be a bit late. In fact, a friend from work came and took a picture of the mounds of snow that lined our little section of the road, which melted each day to freeze in our driveway at night. Don's boss was amazed.

My parents had kindly used an inheritance from my grandmother for me to get us an International Travel-All van, which my Dad had been told was previously owned by some nuns. It was a big, heavy machine.

One morning Don hurried to back out and once again had a struggle. This time, in his efforts, the van slid and became hung up on the small plow that had been used in our little side garden during the summer, but was buried in the snow on the side of the driveway.

Arghhh! He was so upset! He got out of the van and slammed the door. The window broke into a hundred pieces.

Don's lunch was in his hand, and he threw it, as hard as he could, over the roof of the house. As he opened the door of the kitchen shed porch, the top hinge came loose and the door almost came off in his hand! I felt sorry for him—but at the moment the lunch was airborne, I thought "First lunch on the moon!" and had to get busy in the dishpan quickly.

Don went into the bedroom and prayed, with tears, that the Lord would help him with his anger. He never raged at us, but sometimes things would get to him. One time he kicked an air cleaner out of a vehicle, down the yard in anger and broke his toe. It was things like that he asked for help with.

Saturday he was able to pick up another window and install it. Something apparently wasn't right, though, because when he closed the door, the new window broke.

But all Don did was raise his hands and worship Jesus. No anger. He was so thankful because the Lord had helped him with something he really didn't want to be a part of his life.

Another of our favorite car stories begins with Don saying he would be willing on Saturday to watch the younger ones and the boys while I took the two girls and a friend to a ladies' meeting in a nearby town. We went up the two hills to the right, toward the town the children went to school in, with no trouble. At the top of the second hill was a flat open field with no trees on either side. (The other part of the road had been through a small wood.)

The snow had blown onto the road, but was only about a foot and a half deep. I figured with a bit of speed, I could plow right through it with no trouble.

What I didn't realize was that the snow was packed as tightly as the snow the dozer had to bash through—only not as deep. As a result, the car went *thunk*—and absolutely stuck—tight.

After trying to back out, and push with no success no matter how I tried, I decided to walk back and get Don. (Fortunately, it was only about a mile from the house.) He brought our farmer neighbor with his tractor, and the gentleman hooked his chain to the bumper and began to back up. The bumper of the car came off.

Don said, "Looks like my car is coming out piece by piece."

The neighbor replied, "We'd better get bigger pieces than this, or we'll be here all day!"

(My sister wrote this incident into Reader's Digest, and it was published.) And speaking of bumpers—one time Don was towing me in the big heavy International, to get it to start, in the larger town nearby where it had decided to quit. He also had the chain attached to the bumper of the smaller car he was using to pull me. I was quite nervous and afraid I would run into the back of him.

So when we went down a very slight incline and headed toward a traffic light, I put on my brakes, and to my amazement watched the bumper on Don's car curl and peel back like a banana skin! I couldn't believe it! Don wasn't happy—but was his usual gracious self when he saw how rattled I was.

We had a station wagon we had bought way back when we got the insurance money from the car that hit me when we were in the college apartments. It was well-used when we got it, and as time went along, it began to burn oil—then to *really* burn oil!

When Don was working nights and sleeping days, it was up to me to get groceries. That meant I had to use the car, taking the young ones with me.

Before I left, Don firmly reminded me to be sure to put oil in the car on my way home. Dutifully, I watched the oil gauge, and not too far out of town pulled over to add oil.

I pushed the metal spout into the oil can, opened the hood, read the dip-stick, and turned the can over into the "add oil" opening. Ahhh! Success! I did what I was supposed to. Hood down, latched, and off again.

We arrived home about four in the afternoon, and Don was awake. (The older ones had gotten home on the bus. That may have been a factor!) His first question to me as I stood at the bedroom door was, of course, "Did you add oil?"

When I proudly told him, "Yes, I put the whole can in!" his eyes got *big* and a look of astonished disbelief blanketed his face. The can was not a quart, but a gallon! I had put a whole *gallon* of oil into the motor! (But it *looked* like a regular can of oil!) Sometimes my mechanical understanding and capabilities are just amazing!

That car kept running for quite a while longer, and when it finally quit, Don was coming home from work. The man whose house the car stopped in front of came out and bought it for fifty dollars! That enabled us to buy another car from a friend in the Bible study for that exact amount! We were grateful. (But that car, too, was an adventure!)

While we're on the subject of vehicular excitement, let me add one more that our youngest son reminded me of. (This one is a doozie!)

Somewhere along in our string of automotive acquisitions (before the Maverick), we purchased a light-blue-and-white

1967 VW bus. After church one Sunday, we had planned to go to the Pennsylvania Lumberman's Museum, enjoy its history, and have a picnic together.

As we went into the parking lot across from the museum, there was a loud bang.

"The muffler must have fallen off!" I said to Don.

"It's something bigger than that," was the calm reply.

It was the engine! Believe it or not, the engine of the bus had dropped onto the ground.

We stopped, naturally, and while we were wondering what to do, friends (one of the girls from the Red House Bible study and her husband) who were at a music festival that was using the same parking lot came to see what happened. Would you believe he had a long, heavy-duty chain in his pickup and loaned it to Don, who, in his amazingly ingenious fashion, chained the li'l critter's engine into place? So we all went into the museum, enjoyed our picnic, and returned safely home.

What is so wonderful—God's hand in the event—is that our home was thirty-one miles from church, and the church thirty to thirty-five miles from the museum, but the bus didn't decide to "deposit" the engine until we were safely off the highway, where the Lord had the perfect fix waiting for us. Most likely, He had another chuckle over this one, though I can imagine some of the angels were just rolling around in heaven, laughing heartily!

16

More Events at the Red House

THAT HOUSE ON the hill, fondly known as the Red House, was a source of many adventures for us, and many others. When we lived in student housing for the second time, we met and became friends with several Korean students along with the Japanese family previously mentioned. One of them brought his wife and friends out to dinner when we had moved to the Red House. We really cared about them.

But this is really wild. Don was on third shift, and one wintry night, well past midnight, I heard someone calling my name with a foreign accent—right in our living room! It was the Korean students who were friends of the married couple. They had been exploring the area, and gotten stuck in the wonderful, surprising snowdrifts the road abounded in. Needing a haven from the cold, they had come into the house and were calling to let me know and ask permission to stay. Of course, I told them to make themselves comfortable and went back to sleep, not getting up.

When Don came home from work the next morning, he was a bit startled to see me feeding the three young men breakfast along with our children! They were a bit nervous, but Don let them know they were welcome, and he had no problem with them being there. He told me it was because he trusted me, and I am so glad. Rather a wild event, though, hmm?

Our landlord very kindly allowed us to live rent-free in exchange for feeding his animals in the barn each day during the times—fall through mid-spring—when they were in there. During the first summer Don worked on the pole barn (where David fell in the hole) for rent, and later helped build another barn located down in the direction he rode the bathtub.

The boys helped with the haying, which was a big job. Then, when Donny Jr. was about twelve, David ten, and Daniel about eight, they were enlisted to help clean the barn along with the landlord's two sons. The animals had been inside all the months before pasturing, and the cleaning job was several feet deep! The barn was about sixty feet long, and except for the part the hay was kept in, was a major cleaning project. The boys understood that the work paid the summer rent, and bless them, didn't complain. (It's memories like that that make me treasure them all the more!)

A little aside—one time the landlord's eldest son came out to get a drink from the pipe that fed the spring into the famous pond, and I happened to be working in the landlady's garden. Off the top of my head, I called his name and said, "What do you think of Jesus?" I felt it was from the Lord, for it came so quickly, definitely without planning. That evening, Donny asked me what I had said. He said the boy had come back into the barn and begun to shovel feverishly, with each thrust of the shovel saying, "What do you think of Jesus?"

He now has grown to be a very kind professional, and his brother is a skillful and enjoyed teacher. I trust he really does know how much the Lord loves him. Of course, the landlord and his family had been in our prayers, and that He be known is the dearest thing to the Father-heart of God.

Our landlord also had the boys help his sons pick all the green apples of the scrub apple trees and toss them out of the way, so the cattle wouldn't eat them and get sick. One time our neighbor accused the landlord's son of throwing apples at her cattle, and called the police. The son said he had not done it, and that our David was with him. The neighbor said, "Get David, for he will tell the truth." He was brought over, and verified the son's story.

The Bible says, "Even a child is known by his deeds, Whether what he does is pure and right" (Prov. 20:11, NKJV), and "A good name is to be chosen rather than great riches, Loving favor rather than silver and gold" (Prov. 22:1, NKJV). I am so grateful God's mercy was extended to us in this way.

I want to tell one more quick thing about David and our wood stove. One afternoon I had the car and took the little ones to get groceries. The older children came home on the bus.

David decided to make himself a glass of powdered milk, then decided to make it an egg nog by adding some eggs, vanilla, and sugar. Inspired by the process, he decided to add flour and baking powder, and turn the concoction into a cake! For some reason known only to him, he also decided to put green food coloring into the mixture! Then he put it into the cold oven.

When Don came home in the old truck, he started the fire in the kitchen stove, so the oven gradually warmed up enough to bake the cake. But because the heating process was so slow, the cake was, when it was finished, as hard as a brick! It also was a very ugly green!

That didn't seem to matter. For about two weeks, every so often I'd hear the sound of sawing in the kitchen, and one of the older children would be, yes, sawing a piece off the cake for themselves or a younger one. And the entire brick—excuse me—*cake* was eaten, and probably enjoyed!

Another memory of joy, of an event that took place on one of the snowy winter afternoons, involves our son Doug, about four and a half years old at the time. All the children were playing in the living room. The boys enjoyed trucks and cars, and my parents had very kindly sent Christmas gifts of those treasures, for which we all were grateful.

One little aside: our Daniel, who particularly enjoyed farm equipment, had a small working manure spreader, and a little tractor to hook it up to. He was a very gentle little soul, and when I came into the living room one time to see the spreader spreading grass all over the rug, I just didn't have the heart to fuss. To be honest, he really did look cute, so intent and careful to spread just right.

Another time he spread ashes from the wood stove, again carefully and accurately. I just couldn't get upset. He also, as a very little tyke, enjoyed playing "stuck in the driveway."

The driveway of the little house was in the valley between two hills, and anytime there was the slightest melting during the day, the water settled in the driveway, to freeze nicely during the night, as I have mentioned before.

In the morning when he was leaving for work, Don would be playing "stuck in the driveway" on a much larger scale. As soon as he heard the whine of the tires on the ice, little Daniel would be standing at the window watching his father's progress and moving his little matchbox car along the window sill, up, back a little, up a little more, back a little, as he watched his Daddy demonstrate the game in the driveway. All the time, the little guy was making a spinning tires noise with his mouth. He loved the "game." Daddy did not!

But to get back to Doug. He was playing happily with the little gang, while I was in the kitchen starting to get lunch. The Christian radio station, at that time owned by CBN, was playing the song "For Those Tears I Died." Suddenly Doug came running into the kitchen just sobbing. I went to him, sat in a chair, and he laid his dear little head in my lap.

"Nobody hit me, and nobody hurt my feelings. I want to give my heart to Jesus."

What a thrill it was to help him pray and surrender his life to Christ. One never knows what the precious Holy Spirit can use in the lives of our children. That makes the choice of what is allowed in our homes by way of the media extremely, critically important. Even harmless things, deposited in the mind, remain there as clutter and can drown out the beautiful "still small voice" of the Lord, or make the hearing and hungering dull. I cannot emphasize this enough: be careful what you allow in your homes. Of course, as a parent, set the example.

One funny thing happened in the fall of that year. I had taken Donny with me into Wellsville, as I got groceries, maybe to let him practice driving. Always interested in trying to improve our garden, I was thrilled to see that many people had put bags of leaves at the curbs for pick-up. Donny went along with my idea, though a little reluctantly, and helped fill our little English Ford Cortina wagon with as many bags of the leaves as we could stuff into it.

We got home and pulled into the driveway to find Don working on the barn the landlord had him building.

"Hey, Dad! Mom decided to pick up trash in Wellsville so we could start a business."

"What?" Don wondered. What was I up to now?

17

Our Most Difficult Winter

WINTERS, AS I have said, tended to be severe. The winter after the extra children had all gone to their families was particularly difficult. We had not been able to get a lot of wood, so there was not enough for me to cook on the kitchen stove.

We had a wood stove in the living room with a flat top, so I used that to cook, as well as for heating. Because of our budget crunch, we were unable to get propane for the water heater, so every night I would fill our canner to heat water and put it on the living room stove overnight. I also put a pot on the tall old oil heater in the girl's room, and in the very early morning while it was still dark, I would hide behind the heater and take a stand-up bath inside my flannel nightgown.

The kitchen sink also froze, and the kitchen was so cold we had to keep the milk in the fridge so it wouldn't freeze. The only water source that didn't freeze was one line in the bathtub.

I can remember shampoos done on the living room floor with the recipient kneeling with their head over the canner. The children in school had showers after their gym classes, for which we were grateful.

When things began to thaw and the water line from the well leaked, a dear family from the church took all of us in until Don was able to fix the pipes.

When things were back to normal, Joe stopped by and said, "Don, most kids get excited when they get a new bicycle. Yours are happy because the toilet flushes!"

One funny thing I forgot to add—one night during the time that we were staying over with our friends while the water pipes were being fixed, our son Donny and their son were awakened by a bellow that would have made a bull moose jealous. It seems the father was making the rounds to see if everyone was tucked in, and stepped on the plastic parts to the model cars the boys had been assembling on the floor. As a former stevedore, his volume was impressive.

He also had the habit of putting sugar—yes, sugar—on his Jell-O! The children were fascinated to hear "crunch-crunch" as he was eating it.

A little story about a laundromat trip. Don is amazing at fixing washing machines and dryers. As you may remember, he began his training in this career early in our marriage (not by my intention, though) and this capability has proved to be a great blessing, not only to us but to many others. But every so often, the critter would break down, and Don wouldn't be able to fix it right away. When that happened, I would have to gather the clothes, sheets, towels, and often the children and head to a laundromat in a nearby town.

Because I enjoyed giving out tracts (small papers that explain why and how to give one's life to Jesus) and talking to people about the Lord, I would tease and say, "The Lord had the washer break down to send me to the mission field."

On one of the excursions, I met an elderly gentleman, and he shared a story that is quite unique. When he was a young child, he said an old traveling preacher used to come every so often to his little one-room schoolhouse and hold meetings.

One time, the elderly man said, the preacher put an open bear trap on the center of the floor, and covered it with a newspaper. He then took a wooden broom handle, and "walked it" all around on the floor. This, he explained, was what the verse in Hebrews 11:25 meant by the "pleasures of sin for a *season*."

He said, as he walked the stick, "Sin can be fun! And we'll go along enjoying it, but then..." And with that he put the broom handle right into the center of the newspaper and *snap*! The trap took the end right off the handle. "It'll get you!"

What an illustration! Obviously it made an impression on the elderly gentleman who told me of it for he was a boy when he saw it. Various times I have been able to use the same illustration (though I could only get a rat trap), and I hope it was a help to the children who watched it. God's Word is completely true.

One of the winters was extremely snowy. The snow blew across the road and piled into it. When the sun finally came out, we all went out to look around, and were amazed at what we found. Donny found a long stick and stuck it into the center of the road. There, in the middle of the road, the snow measured eight feet! Our oldest daughter tied a bit of cloth on a branch right at the surface of the snow she was standing on. It was fun in the summer to look up in the tree and see where she had been standing on the snowdrift!

The snow that was eight feet deep in the middle of our road was packed so tightly that the snowplows couldn't dent it. It was necessary to have a big Oshkosh Dozer ram and bang its way through! It was absolutely fascinating for the gang to watch.

That winter we were able to get an old toboggan about seven feet long. One Saturday afternoon, Don, Joe, Donny, David, Daniel, and maybe Sam went to test it out.

Up the road from us was a small abandoned farm nestled down in the hillside, a perfect spot. Some boarded, some pushed, jumped on and away they went—then stopped about three-quarters of the way down the hill. When they unloaded to find out why, they found they were on the roof of a small barn that had been built into the hillside! And it would have been at least a twelve-foot drop for them if they had continued.

"For he will give his angels charge over thee, to keep thee in all thy ways" (Ps. 91:11). How kind—and how true!

That toboggan gave us another story. Each fall, winter, and early spring, instead of paying rent, we fed the beef cattle and albino horses our landlord kept in his huge silver barn until the animals were put out to graze. Don would throw down the hay when he came home from the night shift to get it in position to be easily distributed the next day. Then for a period he took a carpentry job from a friend, and stayed in the town where he worked.

Because of that, I would scoot across the snow and duck under the fence to the feed animals as soon as the older children left for school. The little ones were still in bed, or were settled with something safe for the time I would be in the barn. As a city girl who had always wanted to be on a farm, I found the work very interesting.

There were quite a few, maybe thirty, beef cattle and about eight to ten horses. Among the cattle there was a part buffalo bull—named, of course, Napoleon. He was quite a neat guy and loved to have that massive curly head scratched on the front, from above his nose to his ears. I also liked to scoop up the small leaves that fell from the hay—the tasty part, I was told—and sprinkle it over the hay I dished out. Guess my "Momma feed 'em right" attitude slid over into my animal relationships, too.

After a while Don had the three oldest children do the feeding. (I believe it was because I was pregnant.) It worked all right most times, but then there would be—"You mean the bus left already?!" "No, we didn't hear him blowing the horn." (They probably didn't. The barn was a good seventy-five yards from where the bus stopped in front of our house and when you are busy building a hay bale fort it's easy to get caught up in your work.) After a few times of that, I decided that "better late than never" was going to be the motto. So, off they started on the four-mile path down our dirt road to the school in the middle of our little town.

A dear college student happened to be on the roof of the old farmhouse he had purchased up the hill about three-quarters of a mile from us, battling the wind as he tried to tar-paper his roof. He said he didn't know anyone lived on the road until he saw "the troops" coming. We didn't know about him either—just thought some hunters were there on weekends. We decided to meet the "hunters," so I took some fresh-baked something up the hill, and the young man and his bride became close friends with us. Don even helped him build a large kiln in his home for his pottery business. We had happy times together, and started a Bible study one evening a week with them.

About this time, Don noticed a young woman hitchhiking by the road as he was coming home. Fearing for her safety and knowing she would be safe with him, he picked her up and volunteered to take her to her destination in the college town not too far from us.

He began to talk to her about the Lord, and later told me he had never in his life seen anyone get so excited hearing about God and His love. He invited her to come to Sunday dinner and meet his family, and she agreed (though she told me later she was a little unsure of what she would be getting herself into).

She was very pleased to find out about the Bible study, and soon brought several young ladies to join us. They all received Jesus as Savior, to the joy of our hearts, and are walking with Him, as are their families, to this day. In fact, the first young lady met her future husband at a later Bible study in our home when we moved downtown! The Bible study lasted at least seven years, and was a real joy to us.

But back to our bus situation. A few times in the winter the boys missed the bus, but my answer was, "You know the rules." However, since it was winter, I allowed them to take the toboggan rather than walk. When they got home, they said, "The kids treated us like heroes." What I didn't know was that when they went down a good hill—and the little road had several—they would go back up and do it again to make sure it was as good as they thought it was the first time. (Of course! One needs to be sure of an important thing, right?)

And I also didn't know that they would take turns standing watch in the barn until One of them would say, "Yes! He's pulling away!" Then in a few minutes they would act so surprised the bus had left them! What a bunch! I so love them!

18

Mighty Miracles and Great Changes

DURING MY LAUNDRY activities at the Red House, if at all possible, I would put the wet clothes and clothespins on the clean grass and touch my toes with my legs straight as I reached for each item and pin to hang it on the clothesline. As a result, even when I was nine months along in my pregnancies, I could still touch my toes! That's a benefit of having to hang wash for fourteen children, two daddies, and myself of course.

Was I busy? *Absolutely!* But I can tell you from my heart that I'd do it all over again in a *minute*!

That next to last February that we were still in the Red House, child number eight, our sixth son, Dane Peter, was born. Our oldest daughter had a friend staying overnight, so I wanted to have a "girls' day" with them and of course, our other girl, too, so I was diligent to get things caught up the day before.

But in the middle of the night, I was awakened with a telltale symptom that the baby had decided to come! I remember laying there saying, "No, Lord, no, no. Please not quite yet!" But of course, things didn't change.

Don was quite nervous while I made jello to have for the gang and folded laundry and matched socks before I would get into the car. We left a note for the girls, who were old enough to run the house until Don returned. It didn't take too long, and we were blessed with a strong and healthy son.

When Don brought me home, I sat in the living room with the infant on my lap. Son number five, Dale, walked up to me (he was not quite four) and said, "I don't like that baby."

"Why, honey?" I asked.

"He has black hair." (The entire household had blond or very light brown hair.)

"What color is Mommy's hair?" (It was dark brown.)

"Oh," he said calmly, and walked away. He always has been especially easy-going in the family, and I've been told by someone outside of our family who knew him that his kindheartedness was evident even in high school.

I've found that when a child makes a statement or asks a question, it is really helpful to ask them, "Why do you say that?" or "Why did you ask that?" Often, as it was in this case, a "soft answer" not only turns away wrath, but really is helpful in smoothing things out for everyone—including the child. So be careful not to respond in anger, but rather search out the motive. It makes life so much easier!

The next spring Dane was toddling around and already showed a pretty strong outlook on life. One Wednesday afternoon, an older lady friend (not the famous driver) stopped by to visit, with the comment, "I just felt God wanted me to come." By the way, we did not have a phone at this time, nor did I have a vehicle to drive.

We were standing in the kitchen chatting for just a few moments, before I put the tea water on, when I noticed our little son had gone onto the enclosed porch off the kitchen, where Don had some tools on some shelves at the end. When he came back, he was carrying a plastic gallon jug with a little bit of a solution in the bottom. I thought it was some "ooky old rain water" and said, "Give it to me, Honey!" Before I could grab it, that little bugger took a quick, deep gulp—and dropped unconscious on the porch rug!

My friend said we must try to quickly get some egg in him to coat his stomach, so I whizzed one in our blender, and tried to spoon it to him. He was so deeply unconscious, the egg just dribbled out of the sides of his mouth. My friend kindly said she would take me to the little town's medical center. It was well into the afternoon so I explained to our four year old that his brothers and sisters would be home very soon, and left for the doctor's.

The medical center staff tried to give Dane liquid charcoal by mouth to protect his stomach, but it too just dribbled out, his coma was so deep.

At this, the doctor told my friend to put a white cloth out her window (I always used cloth diapers, and had brought a spare) and get to the hospital as fast as she could. When we arrived, they took the little one in for X-rays, and as they were settling him in a crib, Don arrived. Don later told me the doctor called him at work and *over the phone* told him, "Your son has a fifty-fifty chance to live. You'd better get to the hospital." That isn't usually done!

The Bible says "They shall lay hands on the sick, and they shall recover" (Mark 16:18), and so Don, our friend, and I laid our hands on our son and prayed that the Lord would touch him.

At the time, the nurse was taking his respiration count. A normal number for a child his age is twenty to thirty. Dane's was sixty-four, which meant very rapid and very shallow breaths. Right after we prayed, it went down to sixty, and stabilized there.

The doctor joined us and said the X-rays showed that the substance, which he determined to be gasoline, had gone into his lungs (remember the quick deep gulp) rather than his stomach, and had eaten away 65 percent of the lung tissue. He said the hospital didn't have facilities to treat such a case, and made arrangements to transport him to Strong Memorial, a large hospital in Rochester, New York—about a hundred miles away.

They loaded the little one onto a gurney, with a tiny oxygen tent over his head, and we went quickly down the hall and out to the waiting vehicle. When we left at 6:30 p.m., it was the ambulance driver, myself in the middle, Don by the window, with a nurse in the back by the bed. At different times I would signal to the nurse, "How is he?" and she would signal back, "Same," each time.

However, what we didn't know was that our friend had called three churches for prayer for "the Burns baby that drank gasoline." Prayer meetings, usually held on Wednesday, begin about seven o'clock at night and honestly, some time after that I signaled the nurse, "How is he?" and she signaled back that his respiration count had gotten down to forty! That meant his breaths were deeper and slower!

When we arrived at around eight thirty and went to the back of the ambulance, our little son was sitting up, *bellowing* for his mother, and the nurse said his count was thirty-eight! The emergency room at Strong put him into X-ray, and because I wasn't allowed to go in there I could hear him bellowing for me at the top of his lungs! His count was thirty-six! The doctor looked at the X-rays, which showed a little sign of some problem, but nothing major, with an attitude of "What's *this* all about?"

I explained to him that we had seven other children at home, and it would be quite a hardship if Dane was admitted up in Rochester. The doctor told me to go ask the ambulance crew to have a coffee break, which they so kindly did, and he would call our doctor.

Our doctor said, "He's *got* to come to the hospital!"—so we all loaded in for the ride home, and the little one was admitted. I was able to get to see him the next two days, and he was his busy, busy, *busy* little self! At the end of that time, the doctor said, "Take him home! (Did I hear a note of desperation in the doctor's voice?) He's *fine*!" And he has been, too.

One time I was sitting by a swimming pool at a place where our family was camping, and talking to a gentleman about things of the Lord. He seemed very discouraged, and I shared with him the story of Dane's healing. At that very time, Dane—then about six—had begun to jump into the pool, swim across, climb out, jump into the pool, swim across, climb out—over and over again, boundlessly energetic. When I said to the gentleman, "Do you see that boy? He is the one I've been talking about!" his eyes brightened with hope!

We enrolled the three youngest in the school begun by the church we were attending. Dane was so fast and so agile, the school made a rule that anyone aged eleven or older could be on the soccer team with the tall high school students to play against other schools. The head of our school was sitting on the sidelines, and one of the folks from the opposing team's fans made a comment about our "letting the kindergartners play." Our principal said, "You watch"—and Dane just about ran between the legs of the opposition, to help bring our team to victory.

Before he could be on the team, he had to have spikes, so I took him to a store to get some. As he held the spikes in his hands, we talked about his healing.

With our eyes and hearts filled, we shared with each other how extremely kind the Lord was to him—and to all of us—not just sparing his life, but allowing him to burst into action with his wonderful energy. He didn't have to just sit in a wheelchair watching others and wishing he could act like them. The thought deeply moved both of us.

Dane went on to be the captain of the soccer team of his public high school and was one of the very few high school players who could do a "Pele" throw—actually going up in the air and "head over tea-cups." In other words, completely turn his feet up over his head and then fire the ball onto the field when he landed. It was amazing to watch, and the action put a big momentum on the ball.

One thing is for sure, one could not do that with weak or damaged lungs! The Lord was so kind! I can never in my whole life thank Him enough for such a great mercy!

There was one more evidence of His kindness and mercy to us that I don't want to neglect to mention. One day in about my fifth or sixth month of pregnancy for Dane, a gentleman came to our house selling Shaklee vitamins. We told him we knew the products were good quality, but would be unable to purchase any. We wished him well, and he left. But in about a week he was back and said that he and his wife had prayed about it and felt they were to give me the high protein drink for the remainder of my pregnancy!

They did this, and I believe that the strength and abounding energy Dane has had since he was small is related to that. His eyesight is 15/20, which is better than 20/20. I am deeply grateful to the Lord for directing the gentleman way out on our dirt road (don't forget, we were located four miles in either direction from a paved road!) to our home one evening. That truly is amazing!

May the Lord bless that gentleman and his wife in wonderful ways for their sacrificial obedience, reaching out to us with such impacting kindness. Again, I am so *very* grateful. (And doesn't this show the great benefits of good nutrition—even before one's birth!)

We didn't go to a church on Sundays as a family after we were no longer going to the little chapel. We would have meetings in our home with the family.

One time the Lord put a message on my heart based on the story in 2 Samuel 18. Absalom, the son of King David, revolted against his father and attempted to take over the kingdom. In the war, the young man was killed. When the king received the news, he was broken-hearted, and wept as he walked to a room, "Would God I had died for thee" (v. 33). As you read, you could almost hear the wail of "If *only!*" pouring out from the depth of David's being.

I don't remember what I said, but I remember encouraging the family to live so they do not have "if onlys"—and the resulting regrets and even griefs. There must have been an anointing on what was said, because one of the children said, "I had to work all afternoon to take that message out of my mind." But I didn't feel peace not being connected with a church. So on Wednesday evenings, after I got the supper cleared away and things settled, I began to walk the four miles down the dirt road to a prayer meeting at a little church.

The first week there were two older ladies there. The next week the college student pastor gave me a ride home. That Sunday it was Easter, and I just had to go. When I was almost there, guess who drove past me with a carload of children? Don had gotten the whole family ready, and come to church. I was absolutely *thrilled*! And we began going as a family. The Lord is *good*.

God Provides a Home

Don had been working for the landlord (in addition of course to his forty hour per week at the plant) and laid all the blocks for the thirty-by-forty foot foundation for the barn. (He was putting on the flooring when we drove into the driveway with those bags of leaves. He almost fell off from shock!)

Perhaps not realizing how much he was expecting from Don, there began to be a build up of tension between the two. So that summer, we were suddenly given two weeks to leave. I know Don, and I know he didn't "answer ugly" because we had been praying for the landlord and his family and didn't want to cause them to be offended and turn away from the Lord.

So we took a deep breath, and started packing. But we didn't exactly have a place to go. Then the Lord sent a friend who had a small farm (remember the man who loaned us the truck with the smoking problem?), who said he had a small hired-hand house we could use. There was even a garage-like shed we were able to store things in.

Don and Donny took turns driving our old Dodge truck and the big International over to the farm and moving our things, mostly to the shed at first. I kept packing, and would put the things I had gotten ready at the side of the driveway. Because it was easiest, I put our things in large black trash bags. One time, the trash collector came and picked the things up! When Don came back, we figured out what had happened and he made a beeline for the dump. Amazingly, he was able to find our bags of sheets, towels, and quilts—and Donny's electric guitar and small amp!

The little house was a blessing, but it did have its challenges. The former occupant was not too adept at cleaning, so I had to really have at it to make the place livable.

There were two bedrooms—one for the girls, and one for Don and I. The boys slept on mattresses we put down on the living room floor, and stood up during the day. Our friends (the ones that Don built a kiln for) brought over some leftover pinkish paint which we used on the girls' room, and a beige, with which I painted the bathroom. A funny thing about that bathroom: there was no sink, but the absolute longest tub I ever saw. (And it too had "feet.")

We lived there all summer, but with no sign of the next stop. We definitely wanted to stay in our school district, so Don kept looking. Then the farm was sold. That, of course, meant we needed to find another home—quickly. But we were praying and trusted the Lord would provide.

With two weeks to go, my sister and family came to visit, and I can remember my brother-in-law being amazed at our peace. He said, "If I only had two weeks to find a home, I'd be tearing my hair out!" A home opened up for us right in town, which I was delighted about. The children could walk to school, and our church, the post office, and grocery store were also within an easy distance.

The house was an old tannery about twenty-five-by-thirty-feet, two stories, with a bathroom, a small, a medium, and a larger bedroom upstairs, with an alcove at the top of the stairs where Don built two bunk beds for four little guys "feet to feet." There was a kitchen, living room, and dining room downstairs.

When Don brought me to see it, however, we walked on broken glass in the kitchen and dining room. Vandals had smashed the windows (which were boarded up by then) and turned on the faucets for the washing machine hook up. As a result, the kitchen cabinets were all warped and stuck, and things were a big mess! But the landlord made arrangements with us to fix things up in exchange for the first month's rent. We wallpapered the kitchen, painted all the woodwork, and Don planed the warped cabinet doors so they could be used.

We painted the dining room red, and had enough of our red colonial wallpaper to do one end of the room in it. (Our hearts were still on the hill a little, it seemed.) But we were in and settled in time for the family to walk over to school. This began a new phase of life for all of us in town and, would you believe, many more adventures!

19

Fire!

WE WERE IN the metropolis of Andover, New York, population 1,439, and I was glad. I really did love the Red House, and the adventures we had there, but honestly, coming off that hill in the dead of winter scared me to death. In fact, when our oldest began to drive and would give me a ride down to the store, more than once on the last steep downhill curve, fear (or was it sheer terror!) would cause me to burst out loudly praying in tongues!

So being down in town was very much enjoyable to me. However, the friend that Don had helped to build a kiln for very kindly gave Don a plot of land next to his house, and Don had started to build a house on it. He had begun to lay the blocks for the foundation, and had also purchased an old 1952 Dodge flatbed truck.

But we settled in—and it was such a blessing to me to have the children that used to come up to visit at the Red House now come over so we could all pray together before everyone left for school. It was a bit busy, but I really did love it.

One funny thing—to call the children when we lived up on the hill, I would use a yodel-like "Ooooo-ooo, Ooooo-ooo,

Ooo-oo, Ooo-oo, Oooooo-ooo" and could get a good bit of volume with it.

Not long after we moved, the older boys were over on the school ground—just across the little creek, railroad tracks, and the highway from our house. So, when it was time for supper, I called them like I used to. When they came home, the boys said, "Our friends said, 'What's that noise?'" and "We were running a mini-bike and heard you *over* it!" (I was a bit embarrassed—but a little pleased too!)

The children would often come home for lunch, and I would have hot biscuits ready (made as I used to on the hill, with extra powdered milk in them for nourishment.) It was so good to have the extra time together. We'd have that famous "tar pail" full of peanut butter and grape jam as filling, and the children would polish off quite a few before heading back to class.

One day in late spring, I was running a bit behind schedule. The two younger ones had been bathed, but I put Dale in a pair of nighties with feet in them to save a little time, and diapers and a shirt on Dane. As it was a little cool, I lit the small gas space heater in the "big boys'" bedroom, settled the boys in there, and gave them crayons and paper to make some pictures for Daddy. I went downstairs to get the biscuits started for lunch, and shut the door to the steps to keep drafts to a minimum.

I was busy getting the ingredients together, when I heard Dale call me. Little Dane had, as some little people do, the habit of biting if things didn't go his way, but Dale was good at dealing with him—"Naughty baby," he'd say—so I thought I'd let him work it out.

When he called again, I thought I'd better help. When I opened the door to the steps, the air was filled with smoke!

I raced up the steps, and along the little hall and into the bedroom. What met my eyes was unbelievable!

Don had not had time to build bunk beds as yet and the "big boys" were sleeping on their mattresses on the floor. They had used a couple of old sleeping bags (even though they had been asked not to) as blankets—washed so often there was no fire retardant left in them. Dale explained later he was trying to help by keeping the baby entertained, so he put some of the paper into the flame of the heater, to show the baby the "pretty fire."

Apparently when it got too much he had dropped the paper on the sleeping bags and the fire took off. The beds were ablaze, and a pool of flame was eating into the floor. The *noise* was *incredible*! Dale, bless his heart, had not left the room, and when I asked "Where's the baby?" pointed to the crib.

Absolutely, from Dale's first call to my race up the stairs wasn't more than two minutes at the very most. But what I saw nearly made my heart stop.

Flames were shooting under the crib, where the boys had their motorcycle helmets and other things, apparently quite flammable, and up the wall behind the crib, bending as they hit the ceiling! The crib rails at one end had little flames coming off of them—and Dane was standing, holding onto the side of the crib looking at the flames, crying, and jumping up and down!

The Lord is so KIND! For some reason—perhaps someone had wanted to retrieve something under the crib—it was not squarely against the wall, but the end on fire was angled into the room. As I walked around the pool of flames, I could hear my long hair—which I had left hanging loose to dry, melting (a funny, fizzling sound). I went over toward the wall, and reached out and grabbed Dane, who clung tightly as the three of us hurried downstairs. I remember asking Dale "Is Mommy's back on fire?" My hair was waist long and I was wearing a light cotton blouse and skirt so I thought it actually might be. Thankfully, it wasn't.

I hurried the children across the street, opened the neighbor's door, popped them in and said, "Bonnie, call the fire department." With them in good hands, I raced back to turn off the heater, then tried to carry my spaghetti pot of water upstairs—but the smoke was too much. The neighbor's husband came home, saw the flames in the window, and tried to help with his fire extinguisher—but he, too, was driven back by the smoke. Thankfully, the dear volunteer fire department was quickly on the job, and amazingly the house was spared.

When I went back to the neighbor's, the husband said they had taken Dane to the little medical center, because he had burns, so I went right there. His two little hands had burns, there was a burn spot on his back, and one on the side of his nose.

The doctor (the same one who had treated Dane when he drank gasoline) said, "He should be in the hospital, but I know how you people are. But if he can't sleep, won't eat, or won't drink, he has to go to the hospital!"

I said, "I understand," nodding my head in agreement, "but let's give God a try." Also, instead of the doctor giving Dane a DPT (dyptheria, pertussis, and tetanus) shot, I asked if he could only get a tetanus shot. That way his little body didn't have to deal with the other parts of the shot. The doctor kindly agreed. Sometimes we parents must respectfully add our thoughts to a situation for our children.

We went back to the neighbor's house and, when I could finally pry Dane out of my arms, I laid him down and comforted him until he fell asleep on her bed, and he took a nice nap. When he got up, he ate some crackers, and had Kool-Aid. When he joined her son and played trucks, he'd say "hurts" when he pushed the toys around, but still did it.

That night we all invaded the friend's home Don had built the kiln for, as they were away visiting relatives in New York City. We were so grateful for God's mercy, and praising the Lord. Dane was clapping his little bandaged hands as we sang, then held a pen, squeezing it between two hands to draw "gickens"(chickens). No pain.

I was given a prescription for pain pills, and never once had to use them. However, the doctor's office insisted he be given the medication before he was brought in for a check up. And burns they expected would take quite a while were completely healed in less than a week! We were all amazed!

Friends from our little church who had no children took all ten of us into their apartment for several weeks—until we could get the bedrooms fixed in the house. (The husband had an alarm clock that sounded like a bunch of birds awakening. The kids were fascinated!)

It was an absolute lifesaver, and we were so grateful! Thankfully, as I write, they are living in our home while "in between" the one they sold and the one they bought. Because we are at this time living with my elderly mother, we were able to offer them our house to live in and store their things in, and we are very pleased to be able to do so.

A couple of things about this adventure: for one, we heard that many who heard we were having a fire prayed for us, and we are gratefully positive that made a difference! For this reason, whenever I hear a siren, I lift the situation up to the

Lord in prayer—whether it is fire, ambulance, or police, and many of our children and grandchildren do the same.

When we had our fire, our daughter Linda was in about fourth grade, and when she was told, she said, "The Lord will take care of it," and went on with the school activity. Our Donny—then a senior—hurried to the cafeteria to tell the art teacher he was going home because his house was on fire.

The man said "Donny Burns! Of all the excuses I've ever heard for not coming to art class, this one is the worst!" (The teacher didn't believe him!)

When we went back in to survey the damage, we were awed by the obvious hand of the Lord's merciful protection. The heat had been so intense, a plastic swan holding flowers in the bathroom had melted! A little plastic train on a shelf at the end of the hall *away* from the fire *melted*. Don's flannel shirts that were on a shelf in our bedroom, on the wall next to the boy's room were like charred dust when we picked them up. And there was a closet in the boy's room between the fire and that wall!

With the heat so intense, why that old dry building didn't go up like a tinderbox is beyond comprehension. The Lord was so very, very kind, and we were—and are—deeply grateful to those who prayed!

20

Numbers Eight and Nine

We cleaned up, washed all the clothes, bedding, and blankets, and the landlord gave us paint to do the bedroom and hallway walls. Through several unexpected folks' kindness, we again had mattresses for the "big boys," and Dane joined the "feet to feet" gang on the bunk beds in the alcove at the top of the steps.

Our oldest son, Donny Jr., graduated in June. He had been working part-time at the local grocery store and now began to work there full-time. But as I walked down the line to congratulate him at his graduation, I had a secret. When the secret came out, it was really precious to see how everyone was concerned to figure out what would be a good name that started with *D*. It was so cute to see six-foot Donny and his friends in our living room working on the "problem." Donny was quite concerned, for he didn't want the boy to feel left out! (All the other six boys' names start with *D*, as I may have said.)

In late January of 1975, Donny went to visit friends in the New York City area, and came home on the morning of February 11. He said good morning to me, and started to go off to work. Just before he left, I said, "Honey, I might be going to the hospital today."

I had begun to have "rumblings" and would have to hang on as I was mopping the kitchen and dining room during the "rumbles." In a very short time, Donny came busting in the front door. "They sent me home from work when I told them what you said. They said, 'Your mother thinks she is going to the hospital! What are you doing here?'"

I settled Dane with the neighbor, called Don at work, then Donny took me to the hospital—in his friend's car! (Believe me, every time I had a contraction, I'd pray, "Lord, let this contraction do what it should do, but *please* don't let my water break in this boy's car!")

When we got to the hospital and the nurse greeted us, I said to her, "This is number nine, and I think I'm in a hurry."

"Oh, if you are in a hurry, we'll take you right upstairs!" I was whisked upstairs to a labor room and began to get myself ready. I had on one of the long maternity dresses I had made, and a long slip, so I took off the dress and my stockings.

I felt the need to use the bathroom—which was adjoining. I went in, and to my absolute shock, the baby chose that time to come! I rang for the nurse, and just as she came in, the little one made his complete entry into this world, into my hands. "My goodness!" she exclaimed. "Jesus!" I called softly, as I unwound the cord from the baby's neck.

The nurse helped me to walk to the bed, and the doctor came in from another room, all suited up and shoe covers on, to complete the necessary things. The reason I mention the doctor being all suited up is that it is an answer to prayer. You see, I had decided I would have the baby at home, and a friend from the Bible study called around to try to find a doctor that would come to assist. None would.

But then she called a doctor who said, "Is that woman Irene Burns?" When she said "Yes," he said, "Tell her to come to the hospital and I won't charge her." (When I was in the hospital with Dane's birth, I had given him a list of verses from the Bible on marriage, children, and family relationships, but why he connected that request with me must have been the Lord.)

Naturally, I prayed a lot that I wouldn't disturb the doctor in the night, or inconvenience him in any way. So the fact he was on the floor, already ready meant a lot to me.

They moved me to the ward, and in a short while brought our little son to my arms. But he was an ugly purple color. So I closed my eyes, laid my hands on him, and began to pray in tongues. Even though I felt like I wanted to peek, I kept my eyes shut and continued to pray. When a few minutes passed and I felt a release, I opened my eyes. My darling baby was a lovely pink!

Later, a person who came to visit and perhaps to prepare me, said, "Because he was born so quickly, he will be retarded." Something rose up within me, and though I didn't say it audibly, "NO!" resounded in my being!

We do not have to, and absolutely *should not* agree with a bad report! Why "sign the receipt" with our words for something the devil wants to send our way? May the Lord mercifully help us to be alert and careful what comes out of our mouth.

Our son, whom we named Darin Howard (Howard after my father) has been talented and artistic since he was very small and, as an adult, has joined his brothers in being able to play various musical instruments, several self-taught. He also writes songs and has traveled with a music group in the professional music world. The Lord is very kind! I'm so deeply grateful.

One more thing I just remembered. During my pregnancy, I had a great deal of trouble with swollen legs and feet. I knew enough to eliminate salt from my diet, but had to wear the very heavy elastic stockings each day—putting them on after I had laid in bed with my feet up in the air propped against the wall for several minutes.

A day or two before Christmas, a friend and I went to a church in a small nearby city, where they were having healing services. About the middle of the meeting, they began to call out healings as the Lord let them know what He was doing, and the folks would come up for prayer.

They called out, "Someone has been healed of swelling of the feet!" I expected some little old lady to come up front. Then I realized that "little old lady" was *me!*

I went up for prayer, and Christmas Day I absolutely had to go upstairs and take off those heavy elastic stockings, for I couldn't stand to wear them! For the last month of my pregnancy, when I should have had the greatest difficulty, my legs and feet were absolutely normal, with no discomfort. God is good!

21

The Beginning of Testing

ONE WOULD PRESUME that after our fire adventure, the title of this chapter is misplaced. I guarantee, it is not.

While we were still "on the hill," we met some folks that were involved in a group that had gotten into some wrong doctrine. It sounded good, but seemed to put Don under condemnation, not feeling he was good enough, spiritually speaking. There was a real heaviness in their ministry, and I was quite concerned and uneasy. The cap of the situation came for me when we went as a family to a camp they held in a nearby state.

Now, not for a minute do I want to say the people were not kind or very sincere in their love for God and desire to worship and please Him. But somehow the leader got, shall we say, side-tracked, and sadly, others followed.

One of the things they taught was that no church or group had "the truth," and they discouraged attendance anywhere but their meetings. They also discouraged reading any literature but theirs, and were making plans for cities of refuge in Canada, South America, and Ohio.

At the camp, the leader of the group gave several messages. Perhaps when at the moment he said it, Don was distracted, but I heard the man say plainly that at the end of the age "the only Jesus they will ever see is the Jesus in you, and the Jesus in me."

I was aghast! The Bible clearly states that the Lord will come "in like manner as ye have seen him go" (Acts 1:11) and says the same thing in many other scriptures in both the Old and New Testaments. (See Matthew 24:30,44; Thessalonians 4:16; Revelations 1:7; and I John 3:2.) *Very* troubled, I began to seek the Lord, even with fasting, that He would set us free.

I also wrote to a ministry Don respected, telling him my fears. The man kindly wrote back that my fears were correct, and the group was in error. Thankfully, Don agreed. But damage had been done, and the residue, because of his sincere desire for the absolute best for our family, made Don concerned he may have missed the Lord by not moving us to one of the "cities."

The Bible clearly says in Romans 8:1 that "there is... no condemnation to them that are in Christ Jesus. The devil—who is real—does not want us to understand this. He brings us into condemnation when we do miss it, causing discouragement, depression, despondency, and a feeling of hopelessness.

The Lord, however, wants us to repent, receive His freely given forgiveness, dust ourselves off, get up, and go on. And He wants to give us *joy* for the journey!—that our joy might be full. (See John 16:24; Romans 5:1–2; and Isaiah 12:3.) Thankfully, Don has done so, and is fine.

Sometimes it is really hard to get it in our heads—and sometimes it's hard to get it from our heads to our hearts—that the magnificent, awesome Creator of the whole, vast universe, actually *LOVES us*! Jeremiah 29:11 says it so beautifully: "For I know the thoughts that I think toward you, says the LORD, thoughts of peace and not of evil, to give you a future and a hope" (NKJV). Condemnation is a tool of the devil to defeat us, and we need to tell him to go.

Doug Gets Hurt

Our relationship with our precious oldest son had been getting strained.

One thing we did not realize was that he had been listening to a Christian DJ who had an "answering the culture" type show, where he would play a popular rock song, then its "answer" in a contemporary Christian song. We realized the bad influence rock music could have, and deeply longed with our whole hearts to have our home one that the Lord would be willing to allow His presence in, so we would not allow the family to listen to it. (Of course, we didn't listen to it either. A parent certainly must live what he says!) What we didn't know was that our son would record the rock song, and shut off the Christian song. It definitely affected his attitude, and we couldn't understand what was wrong.

One thing Donny did that was really neat was to make our cramped attic into a comfortable loft bedroom. He insulated, put up wallboard, painted, and cut a window in the end under the peak with a chain saw! For carpet, he put various shades of green carpet sample pieces together for a nice effect. Access was a wooden ladder Donny would lower or raise, and he made a carpet-covered trap door he could place over the opening. We all really admired his accomplishment, and Donny enjoyed his space.

That summer the children and I again went up to the camp meeting at the Bible school—of course with neighborhood children also, and our baby whom I was nursing.

One day toward the end of the week, one of the young teen boys who was with us asked me if they could use some of my pots for drums, as they wanted to have a little praise band. I told him yes, but not my cast iron dutch oven, as it would break if hit.

That afternoon, I felt led to go to the missionary service, and asked Doug to put my Bible up in the nursery (where I would be able to listen to the service) while I went downstairs to the ladies' room, with the baby in his basket, and the two younger boys in tow. (Dale was six, and Dane about three and a half.) Two pairs of steps came down the opposite sides of the sanctuary and ended facing each other at one side of a vestibule under the sanctuary proper. The restrooms were on the opposite wall, and along the side of one of the small lobby wall was a large shelf with many pigeonholes in it and a metal pencil sharpener mounted on the side. In the corner next to it was a phone booth.

Dale came out of the men's room and called to me, "Mom! Doug is lying on the floor in a pool of blood!"

What had happened was the pigeonhole shelf had been pulled out on an angle, and Doug had come running full tilt down the steps and into the vestibule. But remember the phone booth in the corner? As Doug tore into the vestibule, he noticed a movement in it, and turned to look. With that he slammed into the shelf, the metal pencil sharpener exactly level with, and smashing into, his left eye.

When I saw him, I was just stunned! He was in a bleeding crumpled pile on the rug, barely conscious. A man carried Doug to the nurse with me, the baby, and the two boys following. She saw right away he was too injured for her care, and called for an ambulance to take him to the large nearby hospital, Rochester Strong Memorial.

Some of the kind campers took care of the two little boys, and said they would also take care of the rest of the children. Another lady took the baby and me up to the hospital to be with Doug. The dear ones at the camp meeting remembered us in prayer.

My heart just ached for Doug. They had him sedated, but it was obvious this was serious. We learned later that there was also some question of abuse! The doctor explained to me that Doug's injury was the same kind they see when one is punched in the eye! (I had not specifically explained about the pigeonhole shelf with the pencil sharpener being out of place, for I did not want to get anyone in trouble.)

The X-ray showed that the cheekbone around the eye was badly fractured, and surgery would be necessary. It was worked out that I would stay at the hospital with the baby in order to be with Doug. Don, of course, had to work, but got the gang and the camping equipment hauled home.

The hospital had a large, almost library-like room to wait in for those whose loved ones were in surgery. They tried to make it as pleasant as possible, and I was grateful. It was also a blessing to talk to others who were waiting, and to hopefully, lovingly turn them to the Lord. Nevertheless, it was such a relief to have my name called and be able to go to Doug's side.

The hospital very kindly allowed me to stay on a little cot in a small room. They also found a baby carriage for the baby, and allowed me to use a shower made for the staff, and a washer and dryer.

Don came up to see us, bringing some clothes for the baby and I. He also brought up some Christian literature, and I was amazed at how the Lord had guided him. One of the magazines had an article about a communist in Russia turning from atheism to Jesus, and amazingly, there was a young Russian nurse on Doug's floor! There were so many other things that just fit and spoke to the needs in the people's lives that I happily thought I was like a pigeonhole desk, myself!

Doug had a dear little roommate with a severe bowel blockage. Surgery was looming, but the Lord so kindly answered prayer, and it wasn't necessary. His mom was *so* thrilled! A little boy in the next room was going to have an IV put in, and his mom said he was very frightened and usually cried very hard during the procedure. We prayed, and the mom said her little son was amazingly peaceful!

God is so kind, and sometimes He put us in situations we wouldn't choose, but where He needs to use us. One time walking out to go down to the cafeteria, I came alongside a young father with his young son. He told me the boy was being discharged after a bout with kidney stones, and was supposed to drink lots of liquids. I shared what I had read in a health magazine: that carbonated water in soda causes crystals in the kidneys.

"Give it to me, Mark," the father said, and the little guy handed his can of pop to his dad without protest. (I was impressed—and grateful.)

When they changed Doug's bandage, or took him to get X-rays, etc., I would go to the cafeteria for a little food. One time as I stood in the checkout line, I gave the woman behind me a gospel tract. Later, when we brought Doug back to Rochester for his check up, we got into the wrong office. There was that woman, and she said, "Do you remember that paper you gave me? Well, I did what it said." I was surprised and thrilled! Not only had the Lord put me where He could use me, He allowed me to see the fruit! What a sweet blessing.

We came home after nine days, and thankfully, Doug had no vision problems. We were very, very grateful!

The Lord had more to teach me through this whole event. Do you remember the iron dutch oven pot? Well, when I was washing the kitchen things we had taken to camp, to my horror I saw the bottom of that pot had a three-sided rectangle piece that was pushed into the bottom of the pot. (It was still connected on the one end of the rectangle.)

Before I go on—the young people at the camp were really *super*! One night, a wind caused the tent of an elderly couple to rip. The kids borrowed needles and thread from as many of us as they could, and laboriously sewed the tent back together. (Back then tents were made of heavy canvas, and it was *no* easy job!)

As for the pot, I was sick, for it cooked five to six of our suppers a week! I set it aside and couldn't even wash it, I was so upset. But every time I thought about the pot—for I knew who had taken it—I prayed, "But Lord, I forgive him!"

This went on almost daily, for months! (I even wanted to see if I could make an exchange with someone with a red geranium in a pot like ours!)

Finally, fall cleaning time came, and in the process, I washed the iron pot. It didn't leak! To make it leak if it was going to, I put water in it, sat it on the stove, and turned the flame right up under it. It didn't leak a *drop*!

"Lord, You've healed the Forgiveness Pot!!"

We used that pot once again for stews, soups, Chinese and Japanese dishes. Then at Christmas time, the dear elderly lady across the street gave us a roast as a Christmas gift. I seared the meat in the pot, then I poured cold water into a hot iron pot, and it broke with a loud "bop!" The brown juice ran down the front of the stove.

"Lord, I broke the Forgiveness Pot!" I wailed.

So I took out the meat, rinsed and cleaned the pot, and set it aside until spring cleaning.

Then, when I washed it during that process—it didn't leak!

"Lord, You healed the Forgiveness Pot—again!" We used that pot for *years*—until it was inadvertently discarded when my dear family surprised me with a wonderful restaurant-sized stove in our "Big House," and the old one with the Forgiveness Pot having been put into the oven by someone, was removed. I was so very disappointed that it was gone!

"But Lord, I forgive them!"

The pot should have leaked the first time, and it *certainly* should have leaked after it broke with the roast in it! Forgiveness really is a very strong force, and it is amazing that the Lord of the universe got involved with our lives, even with something as mundane as a *pot*!

I've shared this story with many, likening the frequent "I forgive him" prayers to the blows needed to drive in a fence post. Hopefully it has encouraged them to persist in prayer. The pot still amazes me. (I *promise* I did *not* ask the Lord to fix that pot!)

22

Children of All Ages

THE LITTLE HOME in town was very enjoyable to me. I used to come down in the mornings, worship the Lord, look out the living room window at the school, and pray for the children and staff. We wallpapered the living room again, after the fire, in a blue and white heather pattern. With the white woodwork and crisp white Cape Cod curtains, it looked clean and nice, though humble.

The heater was on the side wall, and not long after things were nicely freshened up, I noticed a "mural" on the new wallpaper behind the heater. When I asked our three-year-old about it, he shrugged his little shoulders and held out his little hands and said, "Well, I found a pen!"—as if there would be no other use for it! (He was so cute when he said that! I just couldn't get angry with him.)

The same little guy, in his little hooded coat, came banging on the front door, "Mommy! Mommy!" I crouched down, so my head was a little lower than the doorknob, and I would be eye level as I opened the door.

"Mommy! Mommy!"

I opened the door, and said, "I'm not a mommy, I'm a chicken!"

He stopped in his tracks. His eyes went all around my head (looking for feathers?). Then he said emphatically, "You're not a chicken, you're a *mommy*!" (I loved it!)

Another time, he opened the door to go out and slammed it with a shriek! "Mommy, there's a bear out there with a *BIG* nose!" (He held his hands out to the size of a *basketball*!)

Apparently the big shaggy town dog, who was very docile, had lumbered onto our porch just before Dane decided to go out. When he opened the door, the first thing he saw—at his eye level—was the dog's nose! Again, I would encourage young mothers and fathers—please treasure the memories. They make me smile yet!

One last bit of encouragement for parents of young children: have fun, but do not let them win! They really want someone else to be in charge—though they will definitely push to have their way.

This same little energetic, full-of-life boy was told not to touch a visiting friend's "Ray-tar." (The man's name was Ray, so Dane thought his instrument, a guitar, was called by his name. Children's logic is just amazing, and such fun!) Well, of course, that wouldn't do, and after several rebukes I began to smack his little hand—to no avail. Though I hated to do it, I had to resort to what my grandmother used to call "a botch on the barn door"! It took five spankings (and I was near tears) before he would give in and leave the "Ray-tar" alone! I had apologized to our friend, who had offered to move the instrument, but I knew that because the "don't touch" instruction had been given and he was well old enough to obey, we had to win this one. Our friend also understood what the goal was. (The little guy would actually *run* to touch the guitar after he was dealt with and moved away. Whew!)

As parents, we must be sure to enforce our directions with fair, but tangible, consequences for disobedience. Many years later, when we had moved to our present home, the boys owned several motorcycles. The *word* was, "Do not drive a motorcycle without a helmet!" (A sensible, important rule.)

While I was at our sink doing dishes, I looked up to see "you-know-who" (Mr. "Don't touch the Ray-tar") ride a motorcycle out the little dirt driveway and onto the side road, all on *one* wheel, of course! He didn't have on a helmet. In a short while he came back, parked the bike, and headed down to his brothers' auto body shop in our little town.

He didn't come in, probably because he thought I'd ask "the question." (Thank the Lord, as far as I knew, our children didn't lie to us. They may have not *told* us some things, but I don't think they lied. And of course, they knew we would never lie to them.)

However, something needed to be done to show that breaking that rule brought serious consequences. I took my butcher knife, went to the shed, and cut every single wire I could find on the motorcycle. Honestly, though, I wasn't one bit angry. It was rather a cause and effect thing. It turned out later he had used his *brother's* machine! The consequences he faced from that escapade were never discussed. But when one of the boys asked me why I did that, I told them I'd rather mangle that motorcycle than wipe Dane's brains off the rocks in the driveway!

Down to Florida and Back

Early in the summer of the second year after he graduated, our oldest son decided to go with a friend, riding on the back of his motorcycle, to Florida. It would be a twenty-two hour trip. We missed him terribly. That September, for my birthday, the boy sent me a wonderful, very touching gift. He wrote a letter in which he said he knew my heart was to bless others, so he had picked out about twenty pairs of boys' sport socks of different styles and color bandings, for the family. I felt greatly blessed and honored.

At Christmas time he called and asked if he could put a red bow in his hair and *be* the gift he would give to the family, coming home for a short time. (Even as I write this, it stirs emotion in me, making my eyes mist, after all these years—about thirty!) Of course we answered with a resounding yes!

When I knew Donny had left Florida, driving a little blue 1977 Pinto, the Lord put it on my heart to fast and pray for him. When he got home, he told us a story that made me grateful to have obeyed. He said he didn't eat as he traveled, but tried to keep himself awake with NO DOZE tablets. (Whew!) That plan caused him to feel sick, so much so that he had to pull to the side of the road. Friends had given him a rather large faux sheepskin rug, which he spread on the ground and used to sleep on.

When he awoke, there were *ants—all* over the fleece! But only a few were walking across his neck, and there were absolutely none anywhere else on his body. God is so very kind!

Our time together was a treasure, but then Donny had to go back. Just before he left, I asked him how he liked living in Florida. "I hate it," was the terse reply. My heart sank.

He wanted to pick up a sub to eat along the way, and to say "so long" to the folks at the Market where he had worked. When I heard his little car driving slowly up the highway across the tracks from our house, to have one last look before he turned to connect on the road to which would lead him south, I fell on my knees with my face buried in the couch to pray with tears. How grateful I was to be able to ask for the Lord's loving care.

The following summer, our David joined him to work, and after a while, our oldest daughter Laura went down for a short visit. It was there she invented her song, "The Cockroach Yodel." She had sung a small version of it as she kindly did some cleaning for the boys in the kitchen of the small trailer Donny had rented. But the star-studded professional version came when she was cleaning the bathroom before she got ready to take a shower.

When she moved the shower curtain aside to scrub the tub, a huge (fifteen to twenty pounds?) cockroach fell into it. The scream she let out made both boys sit up in bed like the handle of a rake you've stepped on, and they came running to her "rescue." (Needless to say, they didn't let her soon forget it!)

Donny was in Florida for about a year, and when he moved home, that little Pinto was so packed, it even had a complete motorcycle in it! We were so very glad to have him home. When Darin, just learning to talk, saw Donny's fleece, his eye got *big*: "Super-feelie!" (He liked blankets with nap—"feelie" blankets.)

Donny got a job working at the school in maintenance. One night he said to me, "It's always easier to sleep when everyone is home, isn't it?" It seemed he understood.

23

Our Next House on the Hill

DON HAD BEEN working on and had finished laying the block foundation of the house he was building on the land we had been given up on the dirt road the Red House was on. A lady I had met at a rummage sale told me that Alfred University was accepting bids to tear down a large house so that a small terra cotta cottage could be moved to that site. Don bid on it and won. Later he sold some florescent lights out of it and recouped a little more than he bid!

It was a large, older two-story home—built in the 1860s or so—and had been used as an office at the last. The project was *huge*, with only Don, and the three boys, Donny, David, and Daniel, to work on it. There was a time limit, so it meant they had to work evenings, Saturdays, and during summer vacation. It was an absolutely formidable undertaking.

The big, old truck—the 1952 GMC flatbed—was pressed into service and was an invaluable help. Load after load of debris was taken to the dump and wood to the building site. The sides of the building were plank construction—wide boards were placed vertically to form the walls. Lath and plaster were put over that to make the interior walls.

The truck, however, developed a little "personality problem." It wouldn't start. To give it a helping hand, we backed it in on the edge of the lawn of our little house in town, which sloped toward the road.

During the week, the guys would get things dismantled and stacked, but Saturday morning was the time when "old faithful" was to be utilized. When the call was given, "Time to go!", the house would empty, and everyone big enough would get behind the truck and push. At just the right time, Don would pop the clutch, and...chug, chug, chug-chug-chug-CHUG! The old critter would start up, we'd all cheer, "the crew" would climb on and drive off, and the rest of us would go back into the house. That was a weekly occurrence. And it *was* kind of funny!

But by fall the crew was getting discouraged, and the deadline was looming closer. I volunteered to join and help. The house had been shown to me before the project was started. When I got there this time, only the bottom floor was intact, and it was full of rubble.

My first thought was, "Lord! This is what a person whose home has been destroyed by an earthquake sees!" The sight was one of complete devastation, and I found it hard not to imagine that this was all that remained of my *own* home rather than just the near-conclusion of a project. It just took my breath away! Sometimes the Lord gives us just a little taste of tragedy—so news items are not just statistics, but something we can enter into with our hearts.

We kept at it, but one time as the boys took another load of lath and plaster away, the back tires blew! Apparently the tires didn't have quite enough air in them for the load.

The agreement was that we would not only remove everything, but would fill in the hole of the cellar—which was rather large. We were quite concerned as to how to do that, for to purchase enough fill would be quite costly. At that very time, the Lord brought to my attention some large dump trucks filled with dirt from a campus construction project that were on their way to dispose of their loads! The drivers were pleased not to have a drive very far to release their loads, and we were overjoyed. Our need for fill was absolutely taken care of—for *free*! God is so kind!

Don and the boys worked hard building the large place he had designed, and after years, it was all framed, roofed, and studded. The only problem was the longer we lived in town, the less I wanted to move back up on the hill. Because Don had worked so hard building, I certainly did not want to tell him. So I prayed often, "Lord, if You don't want us back on the hill, please change Don's mind."

One Friday evening he and another friend took the boys from Sunday school class to have a sleepover in that house. I thought, "This is it! When he comes home, he'll say, 'We've got to get busy and finish the place so we can move into it!'" To my amazement, he said, "You know, it's a funny thing. I really don't think I want to move there anymore."

Talk about shocked! "Are you sure?" I queried. He was serious! I was shocked and happy! We were able to purchase the little house we were renting, for our kindly landlord and especially his wife wanted us to have it.

The Accident

When Don decided not to move back to the house he was building, he decided to build a trailer for us to use on vacations. It had five box-like compartments on each side for clothes, bedding, cooking utensils, and food. The center was open for the tents. He painted it a warm brown, and it was kind of cute.

Donny Jr. had been working on another Pinto, and on Mother's Day he took it out on a test run with some friends to see a grass fire up on one of the hills. As they were going up a long hill, a family was coming down—way over on his side. Donny got out of the way, and the other car passed safely. But Donny's car began to swerve, and then began to go end over end, landing upside down in a ditch.

We, on the other hand, were eating Sunday dinner. David came home and said, "Donny has had an accident up on Independence Hill." Don and I raced up to find Donny in the farmhouse with his arm being bandaged, while one of the girls was being loaded into the ambulance.

The Lord was so very merciful, and the only injuries were Donny's cut arm and the girl's cut over her eye. We were so deeply grateful—especially when the state trooper commented to Don as the wrecker hauled the crushed remains away that he had never seen a car in that condition after a wreck in which no one *died*!

But there was a little more to the story. (There usually is!) Don had co-signed with Donny for a small loan, so Donny could get his car. Unfortunately, the boy's insurance had just lapsed. For that reason, *Don's* driver's license was suspended for eighteen months!

We had planned a trip to Hershey Highmeadows campground to be able to go to the Full Gospel Business Men's convention later in the summer. That meant—guess who had to drive! We loaded up all the children from Daniel on down—our six, plus four neighbor children—hooked up the brown wooden trailer, headed for Hershey, and set up camp at Highmeadows.

The setting of the convention center was charming, and when we parked the van, Dane yelled, "Mom! There are chickens on the pond!" (They were ducks, of course.) The meetings were wonderful, and then one of the main speakers said he felt the Lord wanted him to call all the children up front to lay hands on them and pray for them. Every child, including ours and the neighbor children, were touched by the Lord in a very tangible way. I was amazed, and so very deeply grateful—especially as during the following years, one of the neighbor girls said that experience helped her believe God was real during the hard times in her life.

Meetings over, we packed up and headed home, again with me driving the van with the trailer in tow. Everything was going along *fairly* well, when Don said he wanted us to take a different route. It seems a friend at work had told him he just "had" to take Route 44 north. The only problem was it went up, down and around, then turned into a dirt road!

When we came down a steep windy part of the road (before we went back up—*straight* up!), residents in the tiny hamlet came out of their houses to see a vehicle come by! I was *so* terrified, and so busy crying out, "Jesus! Help me!" that I didn't have time to tell Don I'd like to squish him like a bug! (Whew! What a trip!)

Heartache Again

One of our sons had gotten into smoking marijuana, though it took a long time for me to realize it—and maybe even accept it. My heart was so very heavy. I remember one evening taking our laundry to the local laundromat, knowing that in the upstairs apartment across the street he was smoking pot with friends. It was hard to breathe, my chest ached so.

A friend of the boys had been put out of his house because of a disagreement with his parents, and we were asked if he could stay with us. We added him to the "big boys'" room, but unfortunately, he had the same "interest" as our son. One night, after they left, I knelt at the foot of a bed and tried to pray—but couldn't. The only sound that came out was deep, wrenching groaning from the depths of my being. (See Romans 8:26.)

Another time a young person from our church and I were showing an evangelistic Christian film in an empty storefront we had been permitted to use. I happened to look out the window and saw our son going into the local bar, followed by his sister in her little skirt-length belted navy coat, with a hood. I wondered if the young person could hear my heart as it shattered onto the cold cement floor.

But there were some funny things, too. One morning when I went in to call the boys for school, I noticed the curtain "askew" and went over to straighten it. What I found was a marijuana plant, about eight or so inches tall, in a flowerpot! The boys lay there stiff as boards with their eyes wide open!

I just plucked out the plant without comment, went into the bathroom, tore it to shreds, and flushed it. Funny thing was, though, I felt no anger and was not upset. Truly, the Lord gave peace.

Later, the friend said, "I see you found our gardening experiment."

"Yes, but there won't be any more, right?"

Another time a friend gave our son a bong (an article of drug paraphernalia) to hide for him. He put it under our little front porch. "No one will see it there," he said.

The very next day, I decided to tidy the front lawn. (Usually, my inside work took all my time—so this was very unusual. A "God thing," perhaps?) It seemed the very first thing I tackled was to pull weeds around the porch.

I spotted the bong—and didn't really know exactly what it was. But it had a funny, suspicious smell, and I didn't like it. So I got my trusty iron frying pan, laid the thing on a rock, and whacked it good. There! Into the trash! When our son's friend complained, he said, "You'll have to take it up with my mother! I didn't do it!"

24

Funny and Fond Memories

WE WERE "ON the hill" (in the Red House) during the 1972 flood. I remember noticing that the little creek that ran behind the old garage was really jumping and wondered why. When Don drove down to the town to get on the highway that would take him to work, he found the road completely washed away by the little bridge. He came back and tried to go the other way, and that, too was washed away.

Our electric went out, so I was thankful to be able to cook for the family on the wood stove. We turned on the little portable radio, and our son Donny taped the local announcer as he relayed the storm's effect on the community.

The small local hospital had a wing built near the river that went through the middle of the town. That river turned vicious and undermined the wing of the hospital! Thankfully, there was enough warning that the patients were evacuated, but that entire wing dropped into the raging waters!

We are grateful Donny thought to record the events as they were broadcast, and later obtained newspapers with pictures. Thankfully the village's recovery was complete, and all is well now.

The Inventor Goes to Work

Across the little creek that ran at the end of our property in town was a little plot of land, and there Don planted a very nice vegetable garden. Our son Daniel, then about thirteen, built a little building there he called a fort. It was about eight feet square. He put a little addition on, which he raised to about eight feet in height. He made it out of old wood he found laying around, and finished the inside with paneling that came from the building they had torn down. He made a little snack bar and a canvas bunk in the loft addition. After a little bit he decided to put on another addition about six feet by ten feet, with a cathedral ceiling.

But no building is complete without an ability to be heated. Dan found a central hot air furnace that had been washed downstream by the 1972 flood. He took the outsides off and got down to the firebox area. He cut a small opening, made a door, and created a little woodstove about two feet square for his fort! Again evident—the extreme disadvantage of not having television.

The next summer he built an A-frame hut for his brothers in the backyard. At first it was about six feet by four feet, then he doubled its length. There was a small brick fire pit in the center, and the hut was covered with old tin Daniel found by the old garage that was on the property. Even as a young teen, Daniel was very creative and industrious.

His brothers enjoyed the A-frame and I believe slept out in it several times. One Saturday morning, I was busy in the cellar with the laundry. When I came up the steps to hang it on the lines, I heard someone splashing along in the creek, going "Oh-oh-oh! Oh-oh-oh!"

It was Doug! He and Dale had decided they wanted to cook breakfast on the little fire pit, but couldn't get the fire to stay lit. Doug got a little gasoline and squirted it onto the embers. With a loud whoosh, the flame traveled up the fluid and onto the leg of his shorts! Thankfully, he had the presence of mind to head right for the creek!

The boys have always been very selfless in crisis situations (like when Dale stayed in the burning room until I could get his baby brother out). When the fire exploded in the little A-frame, Doug waited until Dale got safely out the door before he ran out! (Fortunately the flame was unable to keep going, and the little hut stayed intact.)

I brought Doug into the house and laid him on his sister's bed, where there was more room. There was a blister about the size of my thumb on his inner thigh. I put some aloe vera plant on it and, of course, we prayed. The Lord is so kind. When the neighborhood children came to see him, one asked, "Doesn't that *hurt*?" They were amazed that Doug answered no" The wound healed without infections, and the only discomfort occurred when the bandage slipped when he played. We were so grateful.

Funny and Fond Memories

Like I've said, I really enjoyed the little house. We were right next to the little creek, and our youngest son, Darin—at that time about twenty-seven months old—was delighted to watch the men in charge stock the creek with fish from a special truck one Saturday morning. Then he saw several young boys with fishing poles hurry to try their luck.

I was kneeling, scrubbing out the tub, when I heard a little voice behind me say, "I fishin'!" I turned around to see him with his father's electric shaver cord ready to descend into the toilet! "No, honey!"

Then, a little while later as I was busy putting away laundry in the big boys' room, I heard the little voice again, "I fishin'!" This time he had tossed the little electric alarm clock out the window. Luckily, the plug stayed in, so it could be rescued. Whew!

Darin and B. T. were good buddies and played well together. (B. T., about a year older than Darin, was the little boy I took care of after our daughter went to cosmetology school. He's the one who was hit by a car.) They did take afternoon naps. His mom wanted them to, and I needed them!

After lunch they would be settled in our daughter's room, which had a double bed, and less things of interest for little hands! Then, if they promised to go to sleep, I would tell them a Bible story. A big favorite was when Jesus was in the boat and stilled the storm.

I would go on about how "the rain was coming down, and got the disciples' coats all wet and their hats wet, and the wind was blowing *so* hard [I'd wave my upraised arms back and forth] the waves were crashing into the boat!" (Their little eyes were bright with anticipation.)

"Then, the disciples woke up Jesus, 'Jesus! There is a *big* storm!' So Jesus got up, and stretchhhhed, and yawned, and said..."

With that, two little guys sat right up with their little arms straight out and yelled, "*Peace be still!*" It was *so* cute!

When I told them the story of crossing the Red Sea, I tried to help them see what it was like for the "daddies, and mommies, and children" to walk between two high walls of water! "Here comes a bunch of yellow fish! Look! Here are some big fat blue ones! And see all the little red ones!" Each time, I would move my hand as if the fish were swimming along and made a sharp turn so they wouldn't swim through the wall. To be honest, I had never thought about that before. It must have been really neat! (Funny how the Lord can show you things when you least expect it.)

Speaking of things cute, one time I was driving (probably to pick Don up after work), with Dane in the front seat. We passed a barn with some young cattle in the barnyard.

Suddenly Dane turned to me and yelled, "Mom! That cow *waved* at me!"

The timing was just perfect. Right as we passed, an animal picked up its back leg and scratched its ear! Honestly, I think the Lord enjoyed that, too.

B. T. was also one to speak out, in full volume. (One time he said, "Hi Tim!" to a person on the sidewalk that he spotted out my driver's side window. I thought my head would ring for a week!) But we were walking down the main street of the nearby town, and we passed a man smoking in front of the movie theater. B. T. (about four years old) bellowed out, "Man, do you love Jesus?" The guy nearly swallowed his cigar.

I have so *many* fun and fond memories. Here is just one more. Eugene had gotten into difficulty and again ended up in the county jail. It was a nice spring morning, visiting day, and I had the car. Because it was a little cool and my hair was still a little damp, I threw a torso-length black gabardine cape someone had given me over my shoulders. My hair, as usual, was up in a bun-like thing on my head. Of course, I took the two youngest with me. (Darin wasn't born yet.)

For a treat, I got the boys each an ice cream cone, and we headed down toward the residential end of Main Street on our way to the jail in the next town. Someone pulled out in front of me rather suddenly, but I was able to ease the brakes on firmly. But Dale (then about four and a half years old) was standing in the back behind me, and the momentum caused him to come forward—not enough to be hurt at all, thankfully—ice cream cone first. It hit me in the back of the head and the ice cream ball came off and slowly rolled down my back, as I always sit up when I drive. Mercy!

I was able to pull to the side and retrieve the ice cream ball. Then, thankfully, napkins cleaned up my hair—but the cape still smelled of vanilla. Eugene would have been disappointed if we hadn't come, so we kept going, though the guard did look at me kind of funny. (Was it my hairdo?)

For Christmas of 1976, David bought Dane a green plastic Big Wheel riding toy, and it seems a scooter or some other riding thing for Dale. They were great, and the boys *really* enjoyed them.

But toys *that* good can't wait for spring! So the boys would go around and around our dining room table! Wow!

Darin was just toddling—and one day I heard a "crunch" and walked into the dining room to see him eating a red glass Christmas ball like an apple! God is so kind! I was so grateful to have caught that! And speaking of that table—probably Darin bumped his little head on it, and I kind of brushed it off with a "you'll be alright" kind of remark.

Then I was cleaning, picked up something under the table, and bumped my own head. *Ouch!* "Honey, that must have *really* hurt you!" (Sometimes the Lord has to have us experience something so we can identify with another's pain.)

When good weather came, Dane would take his Hot Wheel way up the hill beside the house, come barreling down that road, and quickly swerve into the neighbor's parking area. It was amazing. He was quite a busy, busy little guy! In fact, not too many days after our daughter and I had wallpapered the bedroom he and Darin shared in our present home, we heard hammering.

Laura and I hurried to investigate, and there were Dane and Darin, happily nailing plastic poinsettias and holly to the wall to decorate for Christmas! We couldn't believe it—and they were so proud. Honestly!

25

Hopes and Dreams

WE WERE A bit "bursting at the seams." One time, I stopped at a rummage/moving sale at a home in a nearby town and asked the lady how many rooms she had in her home. "Sixteen," she replied.

As I drove home, I said to the Lord, "I know You create things like trees, animals, and the like, but not houses. I understand—so don't feel bad, Lord."

Believe it or not, several months later a friend showed us an old former tourist home just outside our town for sale, with twenty-one rooms! Then someone else bought it. Then someone else bought it from them. But one winter evening, Don and I decided to go ask those folks to please call us if they ever wanted to sell it. They said there were no plans to do so, but they would if things changed.

One evening about six months later, the phone rang, and the man told Don that the *next evening* someone was going to put a deposit on the house, but if we could do anything before then we were welcome to try. Don happened to know the name of the president of the little local bank, and called him at his home. The man graciously and kindly said he would take the house Don had been building on the hill as a down payment for the loan—without even looking at it!

We did, however, have to sell the home we were in, which Don told the man he would sell to our oldest son for one dollar. That was OK'd, and we got the mortgage. The Lord is so *kind*!

We were able to move slowly—and of course left some things for Donny Jr., who stayed in the little house. We were able to get things at the "big house" done—floors varnished, windows and curtains washed, and bathrooms and pantry scrubbed. It was a fun time. The vehicle of choice for the move was our big old 1967 Dodge van.

We had the house dedicated to the Lord, by our dear pastor and his wife, who walked and prayed through all the rooms. Afterwards, we and all our friends celebrated with a nice buffet feast together.

Not too long after, our house also provided a home for a young mother and her five children who had been evicted because of the drinking problem of her husband, the children's father. They were with us for a few months, and we were able to help her move into a house she rented and continue on to other steps in her life. It has been a joy to keep in touch with them, and we are so happy the little youngest son has been on the mission field and is prepared for pastoring. The dear mother is a woman of prayer. The Lord can and will bless those who have a heart to seek Him.

The Turkey Truck

Mentioning the old van reminds me of just one more (I promise!) of our "vehicular adventures."

The machine we had before the van was a miniature school bus! It was painted a rather ugly dark green. The passenger door by the driver opened with a long handle, and on the driver's door someone had painted a large fan-tailed turkey! So, of course, it was called the Turkey Truck!

One day in late summer (I believe it was 1974), friends told us we could glean their large raspberry patch. I gathered some neighbor children, a friend with her baby in a basket, and of course, a bunch of our children. All told, we numbered about fourteen.

We climbed the last hill to the farm, and as we pulled into the parking spot, the radiator boiled over, and one end of the muffler dropped to the ground! Wow! I told the children that we'd gather the berries, and just before we left, fix the car after it had a chance to cool.

When it was time, I sent some with empty buckets to get water for the radiator. We filled it, and then I turned my attention to the muffler. I lay on the ground, and shoved that muffler on top of something so it was stuck *good*. There!

But before I got up, our son Doug, then about nine years old, said, "Mother, you can't leave the muffler on that. It's the drive shaft." (Remember—he was nine years old!)

So I reached under again, and put the muffler on something else. While I was busy being a mechanic, I heard Doug say, "Oh! Lisa's bucket!"

Since we had filled the radiator, its water hadn't been needed, and Doug, wanting to get it ready to put it into the Turkey Truck, dumped it—uphill from me. "Oh no!" and the poor little guy began to frantically try to push the water back as it gushed toward me, to no avail.

All I could do was lay there and *laugh*—as I finished "seating" the muffler. I was a mess!

The Turkey Truck graciously dropped its muffler one more time before we got home—but I did not brace it on the drive shaft—thanks to Doug!

Well, to be honest, there is one more adventure that I feel is too important to omit because it showed me in an astounding way that God speaks, protects, and cares about things even when we are totally unaware of dangers.

One late afternoon, our oldest son came into the house with his face as white as a sheet, looking frightened. "Mom, does God speak through dreams?" he asked. I replied, "Well, honey, the Bible says He is the same yesterday, today, and forever, so I'm sure He does." (See Hebrews 13:8.)

Donny went on to explain that he, three friends, and his brother David often went to the nearby college, where they would shoot hoops or swim. Then they would all get into his little blue Pinto and head back. Part of the trip was down a steep, winding dirt road, which would cross railroad tracks at the bottom before ending at the small highway leading to town. On the right just before the tracks were two metal sheds, one larger than the other, which contained power equipment either belonging to the natural gas supplier, the electric company, or perhaps the railroad. Donny said that when they came down the hill, they would go as fast as they possibly could down the road, shoot across the tracks, and then onto the highway.

However, the night before, he had dreamed that as he and the guys were coming back from one of their usual trips to the college, speeding very excessively down the road, they reached the bottom of the hill to discover that there was a train going across the tracks. To avoid hitting it, Donny swung to the right and hit the largest shed. It exploded and burst into flames. Several of the boys were killed and he was very badly burned.

Earlier the next day—the day he came to talk to me, pale-faced—he told the dream to the first boy he picked up on the way to the gym, and as they began on their trip down the dirt road, this boy asked Donny to tell the dream to the guys in the backseat. Because he was busy telling them the dream, he was going a moderate, sensible rate of speed. That was the only reason he wasn't speeding, as they usually did. When they got to the bottom of the hill, to their absolute astonishment and horror, there was a train!

What a kindness of the heavenly Father to warn Donny so strongly! Each time we drive past those sheds at the bottom of the hill, my heart fills with gratitude beyond expression. The Lord is so very merciful and has been so to us. How can we *ever* thank Him?

26

The End of the Matter

THE LORD HAS been so very kind to us, and Don and I are more grateful than we can put into words. The Lord has kept His loving hand on each one of our children, and they are all now walking with Him. What a *priceless* blessing!

Because of all the Lord has done, I would like to sum it all up. It's hard to put so many years of living into a few paragraphs, but I will try to condense things, and yet be inclusive. I trust what follows is an encouragement and brings hope to you. There will be many events, joys, and tears omitted. But I trust the Lord's mercy and care will be seen. Believe me—without that I don't even want to think about it.

Here goes—from the oldest to the youngest.

Number One

Our firstborn, Donny Jr., went to the same college as his father, received a scholarship from Kodak, graduated twenty-seventh in a class of around seven hundred, and went to work for Kodak in Rochester. He married a lovely girl he met when he worked at the high school, and they have two children—Angela and Nicholas.

He worked at Kodak for nearly twenty years, then he and Sue felt the Lord leading them to move to North Carolina.

He was in a management position, very well-liked, and Kodak offered him a 50 percent raise to stay. Thankfully, they obeyed the Lord, and after they had lived down South about two years, Kodak closed his division. We were all amazed.

Donny designed and built a beautiful home, and then another one on the lot next door. He contracted out the framing and some other parts of the project, but he and his dear family did most of the work. Of course, the rest of the "gang" came down to help any time possible.

I want to mention one thing to show what kind of a person Donny is. Donny and Sue rented a house while they were building their home. The Lord was so very kind—and the house was right across the street from the house of his brother Dane and his family! What a *joy*!

Well, the house had been owned by an elderly lady who seemed to have had the idea that the kitchen sink drain was where one disposes of grease. Inevitably, the sink wouldn't drain at all. They called the landlord, and he said he would send his son, a thirteen year old, to fix it.

Donny didn't want the young boy to have to work on such a project, for he would have to go under the house in the crawl space. In the south, such places are not very pleasant for humans, but critters of all kinds find them delightful. (Thinking of it makes me shudder, and I appreciate Donny's kindness, wanting to do a very unpleasant job himself rather than have that boy go through it.)

So, after working on the new house all day, Donny came home and stuffed his six-foot-two-inch frame under the rental house into the crawl space to try to open the drain.

He succeeded, and it opened—but let go all over him! He put the line back together, and came quickly up and inside to the bathroom—to find his son and daughter giving the family's beagle dog, Champion, a bath! Donny told the children he would take over, and he and Champ would shower together. There were *two* Champions in the shower that day—and one is a champion of kindness!

Sue had gotten her master's degree while they were still in Rochester and taught as a guidance counselor in a large nearby middle school. She now works as school relations coordinator and continues to touch many young lives. Angela was nominated as "First-Year Teacher of the Year" for her county. She is also the special education teacher. She teaches special needs children, loves them, and touches many lives also. She sings and led a large children's ministry at the church. A dancer, she also choreographs the programs.

Nick graduated, is doing well, has a band, and is a graphic designer. Donny runs sound for the worship team in their church, and he and Sue have opened their home to many groups, including having a dinner for sixty or more college students every Tuesday evening during the school term. Donny and his brother Doug had a business together, "Mr. Rebuildables," a real blessing and help to many. He now works as production manager for a company that produces rebarb, the metal bars put into cement for strength).

One thing that really should be mentioned: when we lived on the hill, Don got a red Ford Falcon station wagon. It ran for a good number of years—with the two engines and three transmissions, and two rear ends that were put in it, as I have mentioned before.

Donny, being the oldest and therefore able, was enlisted to help in these projects, bless his heart. (*Never* heard him complain!)

The "events" were done in the driveway, and Donny remembers the car being put over the cellar way more than once, so it could be worked on. (Sort of a homemade lift.)

That was hands-on training, and while Donny was in Florida, he learned auto-body work and painting. These skills he has taught all the boys, in sort of a domino way, and they have all used them gratefully and very well.

Number Two

Laura worked after high school as a live-in nanny until she went to cosmetology school. She got a job in the small village nearby, and a little upstairs apartment there. Don stopped by to see her with the little boys, and Dane came home and excitedly announced, "Mom! She hasn't wrecked her bedroom yet!"

In time she purchased a home, then went into cosmetology business with a good friend. She married a nice gentleman with a young daughter, Gillian, who lived with her mother. Mike and Laura have two daughters: Alicia, who is a physician's assistant, and Sarah, who is in college studying.

Alicia is the one who has so kindly deciphered Gramma's "whirly-gig" handwriting and put it all into typed—and therefore legible—sheets.

The Lord opened the door for Sarah to be a part of the Integrity Music Kids' CD *Shout to the Lord*, along with her cousins (whom you will meet later), through a friend of the family, Ami Sandstrom. Laura has taught Sunday school, children's church, and Pioneer Club (a Christian's children's group) for years, and has just been a beautiful help and blessing to the whole family, as has Mike. They are dearly loved by all of us, and greatly appreciated and respected in the community.

Number Three

The Lord has been very kind to David. While in high school, he was captain of the soccer team. (One time, when a teammate made a glaring error, David jokingly called out, "Use your head for something besides a hat rack!" The laughter that followed thankfully brought relief to a stressful situation.)

When he and his brother Daniel were together on the team, it won the championship—unbeaten and un-scored-upon all season! The year, I believe, was 1976. He also made two huge plaques—one of a stylized eagle, and the other a panther's head, which hung in the school auditorium for at least twenty years. He ran track with much success as well. He was in a rock band, and then started one with his brother Daniel as lead vocalist. Donny ran sound, and at times played bass with them. David played guitar and has taught himself banjo.

They were very successful, but I just couldn't go to hear them. Sometime along in this journey David began to cough up blood. (He didn't tell me until quite a while later.) He thought, "Why am I doing this to myself?" and quit smoking completely! Just like that. *Praise God!*

He has two sons, Jason and Matthew, young adults and very nice young men. Matt's *little* (graduated twenty-one students!) school went all the way to the Glen Falls high school basketball championship and were defeated by a school from New York City in the final game, by one point!

Jason and Matt are both doing well in college.

The rock band disbanded, and after a few different jobs, he and his brother Daniel formed Mr. Goodbody Auto Sales and Service in our town, and purchased the building.

David turned back to the Lord, met a wonderful girl, Billie, bought property on the road "the Red House" was on, and designed and built a wonderful timber-frame home with a large deck. They had a lovely wedding in the home, and have four precious children—Rebecca, Rachael, Renae, and Ryan Daniel. Billie works at the university as the secretary for Undergraduate Scheduling and Administrative Advising.

David leads worship in his church, and he, along with his father, son Jason, brother-in-law, and four friends, have a gospel/Dixieland band, Brother Dietze and the Dixie Boys.

Before I move on, though, I want to mention something that shows more of the kind of heart that David carries in his chest. The first winter we were at our "big house," David had a job at the milk processing plant in a town several miles away. Because he had been having car difficulties, he had been told, "Be on time!"

One cold, windy day, his car just would not start. He was on second shift, so little Darin—then about three and a half years old, was busy at the "coloring corner." When David came into the house, hands aching and cold, knowing he might lose his job, little Darin came running up to him holding up a picture.

"See what I made."

Ruffling his little brother's hair, David said, "That's really great!", taking time to give the little one his attention and encouragement. He then went in to call the dairy. I was so touched that David, in spite of his physical discomfort, tension, and stress, would not take it out on Darin, or even say, "Don't bother me now." That kindness is a very strong trait in David, and still is. What joy that brings to us!

Number Four

Child number four and son number three is Daniel Thomas. His name is very fitting, for he is a man of integrity and prayer. He never complains, and I have never, ever heard him say an unkind word about anyone.

After he graduated from high school (and by the way, he too was co-captain of the soccer team), before Mr. Goodbody got going, he worked at the market in town. During that time he made absolutely beautiful carvings that are like paintings with the objects standing out, and then painted as if they were paintings. (His subjects are trees, flowers, trains, rocks, etc.) He sold a few, but I am grateful to possess the first one he did—in eighth grade—a farm scene, on display in our kitchen, and a lovely field and well scene that is displayed in our living room.

He met and married a very nice girl, Elaine, who works as a bank teller and has additional training in banking. They have four super children. Their daughter Danielle graduated from college as an English major and now works as an executive search consultant. Dustin graduated from the "Tech" with a business major. Amanda attends Houghton College, majoring in Special Education, and Alexa is in eleventh grade.

These girls, and Donny's daughter Angela, all took part in the *Shout to the Lord* projects by Integrity Music through a family friend, Ami Sandstrom, along with, as I mentioned before, Laura's daughter Sarah.

Dan has always been a very creative hard worker. He designed, supervised, and of course, built a wonderful and completely house-changing addition for his sister Laura's home, and designed and built the hairdresser shop that Laura and her sister own. Then he turned the large, empty upstairs into a very cozy and pleasant apartment for our other daughter, Linda, right above the shop.

He also "inherited" the "little house" when Donny moved to Rochester, and after laboriously pounding out a million nails in the boards left from the house we tore down, built a wonderful sunken family room, enlarged three bedrooms, rebuilt the bathroom and added another—mostly single-handedly—on that house. Then he remodled their kitchen.

Daniel started hosting a prayer breakfast in his home—which now is held up at David's—and on Tuesday mornings goes into his church for six o'clock prayer. He often sings on the worship team. He is serving his second term on the school board, helps design and build sets for plays and video records events for the school. He is a real blessing to the community and to our family, and is greatly admired and respected by all who know him. The village chose him as their Man of the Year in 2005, and he and David were honored as Business of the Year in 2003 for their Mr. Goodbody enterprise.

Number Five

Linda is the "pickle in the middle" (i.e., number five). She was quite an artist in high school, sang in all-state choirs, was in the marching band, and was captain of the cheerleading squad. After graduation, she went to the same cosmetology school as her sister, and joined her in the business.

She very kindly completely redecorated the living room in the "big house" for us, as a surprise. (Don took me to Rochester to stay overnight at Donny Jr.'s.) She bought curtains for it and the kitchen and surprised me with a very large set of charming strawberry-patterned Corelle ware for Christmas. The girls had given me old-fashioned, red-checked wallpaper for the kitchen, and with the red woodwork and white curtains—it is so cute!

Linda also redecorated her bedroom, and found neat perfect wallpaper at one dollar a roll for our large hall. We are very grateful, and it certainly gave the place a boost. With her brother's help, Linda turned the bathroom (with the tub with feet!) into a charming country style, blue with tiny flowered and striped wainscoting.

Later, she moved into the apartment above the hairdressers, and married a nice young man named Shawn Derrick, who plays drums and keyboard in the Dixie Boys and also played keyboard in a Christian group David had formed for a while. They have since purchased a house. Shawn works in investment real estate.

One thing that Linda did was to meet a young man connected with dc Talk in a store in Toronto. It was a case of the Lord having her in the right place at the right time. From this meeting, Doug, Dane, and Darin got jobs traveling with them and also with Stephen Curtis Chapman, selling merchandise. It was quite an adventure and experience for them! Linda and Shawn both sing on the worship team in their church, and we praise the Lord for their walk with Him.

Number Six

We're getting there!

One time when the children asked me what was for dinner, I said calmly, "Baked sneakers."

"Mother!"

Don't forget to have fun. One time as I was putting on a bunch of little coats, I said, while helping an arm go in, "Put your nose in here"—and indicating the other arm—"and your ears in here!"

"Mommy! *That's* not my *nose*!" It brought giggles, and turned something that could get a little tedious into fun. Now I do that with our grandchildren, and tell them, "I used to do that with your Daddy (or Mommy)." They enjoy that!

Now for number six—our Douglas Stephen.

Doug had met an exchange student from Mexico, and after high school graduation, decided to go to California with him to enroll in a school for rock performers. (Doug had also been captain of the soccer team, by the way.) The night before he left, he came and sat next to the chair where I was sitting reading my Bible.

We talked quietly, and I must admit tears ran down my face. The next morning, as he was leaving, he said, "I wonder what's the rush to go."

Of course, the Lord heard about his trip a *lot*, and for some reason, things didn't work out at the school, or with the friend they were to stay with there. Doug's friend invited him to go to Mexico with him. The boy had to bribe his way into Mexico, and Doug became uneasy. After a short visit with his family, Doug decided to head back, and Horatio wanted to go, too.

At the border: "Why are you going into the U.S.?"

"Where are you going?"

"Do you have a job?"

"Do you have a residence?"

He was really worried! They weren't going to let Horatio back in to go to Los Angeles.

It took *twenty-four hours* of investigating! The car was searched thoroughly, and finally they were released to go. Doug took his friend back to Los Angeles, and then headed straight for Andover. God is so *kind*!

Doug went to Fredonia, where he majored in sound recording, auditorium audio, and music in general. He is very gifted. He met his lovely wife, Laura Elizabeth, at college, and they have two children—Benjamin, who looks so much like his dad at that age—it is wonderful—and Olivia, with her mom's pretty brown eyes. (From Gramma's perspective, *all* our grandchildren are adorable, and these are no exception!) Laura Elizabeth is a school librarian and enjoys her work with the children.

They are very active in their church, and Doug plays guitar on the worship team. They have their home also in North Carolina. Doug now designs sound systems for churches and supervises recording.

Number Seven

Hang on—there are just two more to go!

Before continuing—the reason to include various details (and adventures) is to display the Lord's mercy and care. He is no "respecter of persons," and even when the road turns rough and bumpy, He will be there for *you* as "a very present help in trouble" (Ps. 46:1).

The Lord, in His kindness and mercy, will even do things for us when we don't know we need to ask His help. Some of the boys did some very foolhardy and dangerous (to themselves) things with vehicles, which I found out about many years later. Totally unaware of what they were doing, I surely was not praying about their activities—but I'm also sure the Lord must have sent special (and strong!) angels for their protection! Be encouraged! And speaking of angels—can one more car adventure be squeezed in here?

The children and I had been out again gleaning berries, I think, in a car whose hood latch had been broken. Don had tied it pretty securely, but somehow the rope broke, and *pop*!—up went the hood in front of the windshield.

It's a little hard to drive like that, so I eased to the side of the road to fix it. When I got out of the car, I inadvertently shut Dale's little hand in the car door! I felt so very sorry for him!

We didn't have any water, or anything to bring comfort to the dear little fingers. I said to the children, "Let's pray!" Within a very short time, the tears were dry, and Dale was just fine! God is *good*!

The next thing was the hood. (It actually did the same thing to Don and Ray—of Ray-tar fame—when they were driving up to Bible camp. That time it lifted and then sailed over the car like a big Frisbee! Wow!) But back to us. The hood lay flat again with a little help, but somehow the rope must have fallen off, for there was only a little bit to work with.

I told the children we had to ask the Lord to send an angel to sit on the hood and hold it down for us. You know, it seems He did, and a rather large one too, for the hood vibrated *much* less than when it was secured by ropes! Wonder what that angel thought of *that* assignment? When his friends asked him, "What did you do today?" did he tell them, "I was a hood ornament"? I hope to ask when I get there!

Now back to number seven, our Dale Jonathan. In case you haven't noticed, there *is* a pattern here. All the boys' names start with *D* and the girls with an *L*. It does make it easier when marking boots and other items for school, and handing them down. (Just kidding!) You've already met him a little.

After high school, he went to the nearby university, where he had received a scholarship. But according to him, he hated it. Rather than have him continue in something he was so unhappy with, I suggested he take a sabbatical, pray about it, and the following year he'd know what he was to do. Funny thing was—he had been given a word at his Christian high school graduation not to "do what looks good in man's eyes." Because the university had a prestigious reputation, some of his siblings, especially, encouraged him to go in that direction.

So, for a year he worked with his brothers at Mr. Goodbody. The following fall he entered the State Tech at Alfred, taking electronics, and was a part of the charter class to be four years in length for that course. To his surprise, however, he found that the material taught at the Christian school by the pastor of our church, who had been in electronics in the British Air Force, had been so advanced that he was able to coast for quite a while in his college electronic courses.

In his last year, he worked quite a few hours in the computer center, and at graduation was hired there, working several years. He then went to an industry in a nearby city and worked for about two years, then was asked to return to the computer center. He wouldn't bring it up himself, but the college was very sorry he had gone to industry and was extremely glad to have him back! He now works as network manager for Alfred State College.

He had met a lovely young lady named Amy while in college, through our daughter Linda. Upon Amy's graduation, she worked as an adjunct professor of introductory chemistry and biological chemistry.

Dale and Amy enjoyed each other's company for about a year—then Amy's father, a professor at the college said, "No phone calls, no letters, no seeing each other at all for a month. Each of you pray and find out what the Lord wants of this relationship." I really admire him for this.

When Dale told me, he was very sad. "She's my best friend!"

Now one factor that is important is that Amy's last name was the same as ours: Burns. We are probably very distantly related through the poet Robert Burns, but otherwise not at all.

One evening as Dale was praying he asked the Lord for a verse. He opened his Bible, and his eye lit upon the last part of Numbers 36:6. (Now remember that Amy's last name was the same as ours.) "Let them marry to whom they think best; only to the family of the tribe of their father shall they marry."

This was the answer Moses was given by the Lord to settle the concern that land inherited by daughters in one tribe might be lost through marriage into another tribe. (Each tribe numbered thousands—so there was no problem with such marriages.)

When one considers how many zillion verses there are in the Bible, the fact that Dale opened the Book to that verse is rather remarkable, considering both last names were the same. Mr. Burns accepted the scripture as a word from the Lord, and they had a lovely wedding, with everyone in the bridal party bearing the last name of Burns!

Dale bid on a little house that was up for tax sale, but because of broken pipes, he had to completely gut and renovate it. It was a lot of work, and both families helped, but they came home to a charming little place. The Lord has since blessed them with three sweet girls, Natalie, Megan, and Lauren; a dear little boy, Zachary; and a baby named Jennifer. They have moved to a house in the town nearby, and are very active in their church. God is so *kind*!

Before I go on, maybe I could pop in one more car adventure, just to lighten things up.

When the van "retired," our son Daniel very kindly bought us a brown Maverick from the man down the street for about fifty dollars, so we had wheels! The car was a blessing, but had, and developed, a few "personality problems"—the radiator being one of them. One time, because we really wanted to go to the evening service at our church, we filled up twenty-one empty milk gallon jugs with water—and got there!

However, the car must have been annoyed being kept out late, and the twenty-one refilled jugs were not enough to bring us home the thirty-one miles. We had to stop and fill up jugs at a small creek to make it back! But the most outstanding adventure it gave us was when we were taking the three boys to pick up their ride to the Christian school. As we rounded a small curve leaving town, the transmission froze solid and we cleaned off a family's mailbox to the ground! Now *that* was exciting!

The family graciously let us call the boys' ride, they had a day off, and Don made compensation for our mailbox chop-job.

Number Eight

Number eight, Dane Peter.

The summer between his junior and senior year of high school, he started a painting business, painting his sisters' hair salon, The Hairdressers. It was very artistically done, with light and dark turquoise, and light and dark pinks, bringing out the decorative way the older building was built. The next summer, he, a friend, and some of his brothers painted a jewelry store the same way (different colors) and a house, emphasizing the gingerbread. (It was really cute.) He and a friend also painted a large billboard for a local restaurant.

It was while he was working on a project that he and his friend drove into a small city east of here.

"Stop the truck!" Dane yelled to Mike. "Park."

With that, he hurried into the drug store, grabbed two packages of gum, threw them on the counter and said to the young lady at the counter, "I want you to go out with me!" He looked like a rough character: work boots, cut off jeans, sleeves cut off his sweatshirt, and a bandana around his head.

"I will *not*!" was the prompt reply.

About three months later he went back, dressed respectably, and asked again.

This time, Neva said yes because she was leaving in two weeks to go to Florida to live.

During those two weeks, Dane won her heart, then he went off on tour (with his brother Doug, selling the merchandise for dc Talk), and Neva moved to Florida. As soon as the tour ended, Dane took a friend and drove to Florida to convince her to move back. She did, and they were married in a beautiful outdoor setting.

That November, they decided to move to Concord, North Carolina. (They were the first of us to go.) That trip was an *adventure*, and God's protection was very evident.

Dane drove an old bread delivery truck—his work truck—with all their house plants in the front. (He looked like he was driving a jungle!) Neva drove their car with their golden retriever; Don drove Dane's little pickup, and I drove the car we'd come home in. It was a long trip—seventeen hours—and near the last mile or so, I awakened heading toward a big log truck in the other lane. (Now that will make you sit right up!)

Dane continues with his painting business, and he and Neva have two super (of course!) children—Jack Tucker and Eliza Dane. They both are very active in their church. Dane plays bass in the worship band and can play piano and keyboard. At times he and Neva (who also is gifted on piano and keyboard) duet. The Lord has done a *great* work!

Another thing that makes my heart sing that pertains to Dane: Dane had taken his small son, Jack, and Abby, a family friend in her twenties that had been staying with them, on a picnic to a little lake. Jack was standing at the end of the dock, and Dane went to pack the car, which was parked by the dock, while Abby folded the towels. Out of the corner of his eye, he saw the top of Jack's head under the water. Dane's speed kicked in, and racing down the dock, he jumped into the water. He found Jack and heaved him above his head to safety. (Whew!)

Later, Neva asked her little boy, "What did you do, honey, when you were in the water? Were you afraid?"

"Well, every time I touched bottom, I jumped as hard as I could to get to the top," was his reply.

Amazing! Jack had touched the bottom four times, each time causing him to go out farther from the dock.

Explaining Our "Car Philosophy"

As I have said, Don, bless his kind heart, always wanted to have nice vehicles for the family, but we really felt the Lord did not want us to go into a large debt to get one. As for me, the Lord has blessed me with an attitude of, "If it has four wheels on the bottom, and one inside to steer, and runs—what else is needed?"

So, because they are funny to me, and I hope to you also, here is just one more (I promise!) car adventure. Knowing the brown Maverick was done, our son Donny got a little red Subaru wagon in Rochester—I think for about fifty dollars—and gave it to us. It was a real blessing, economical and could fit the family, for we still had four boys at home. The only problem was that the floor was rusty, and rusting.

One Sunday morning, when it was raining, Don went to kindly move the car out of our puddle-filled driveway to the end of the sidewalk for us. He came in *disgusted*! He drove through one of the puddles, and the muddy water splashed in, hit the ceiling and came down on his tie!

One time we asked the boys in the back what they were doing. It seemed they had moved the rug and were sharpening their pencils on the road as we drove along!

The Lord did use it, though. We had invited a family from church who stopped in to stay for dinner. Don said he would go get milk, and the guy said he'd like to go along.

When they got back, the gentleman said, "I was depressed about my car, but not anymore!" He sat down in ours and his foot went right through to the ground!

But the story doesn't stop here. There was a lady's prayer meeting in the next town, and when I met one of women, she said, "I've been praying you'd have a new car—without any payments."

That is just what happened! Our dear family got us a nice green station wagon, and fixed it and cleaned it down at the body shop. Then one day—perhaps for my birthday—they brought it up to the house, and presented it to us.

Believe me, I cried *very* hard! I was *stunned* at the beautiful answer to prayer—filling a need I hadn't even mentioned to anyone. Amazing! God is so *kind*!

The sweeties gave us several other cars after that. Most recently, a few Christmases ago, the family all contributed, and the Carolina boys gave a beautiful red Ford Taurus they had fixed for us. They parked it in the front yard, with a huge golden bow on it! What a surprise! Truly, Don and I are very, very, *blessed*!

Number Nine

Darin was three when we moved to our present home. He has always been very creative (the dangerous effect of no television). One time, soon after the move, Don brought quite a few empty cardboard boxes home to organize stuff the next evening.

During the day, a sawing sound came from the living room. Darin had a serrated knife and was busy making things with the boxes. Honestly, he made an ice cream stand, a helicopter, and to top it off a little race car with a door on the side with a screen door spring so it would swing closed! Was his father surprised when he saw the boxes!

The three youngest went to the Christian school hosted by our church, and I am so thankful for that impartation to their lives. It was worth every bit of the struggle. (Transportation was a big issue, and finances a factor also.)

Darin went there until the sixth grade and Dane was in ninth and then began public school. The difficulty with transportation was a big factor of their decision to leave the

Christian school, and I felt very badly about it. I still am so very glad they went there for as long as they did. I helped out with the art program where needed and have many wonderful memories of the Lord working with all of us—children and faculty. He is a treasure beyond all measure!

Both Dane and Darin had to go back for a Fall semester to take a course they did poorly in, because of incomplete assignments, before graduating. Some of the family wanted Don and me to speak to the teacher to "up" their grade, but we felt that we should not. Sowing and reaping the consequence—good or bad, is a good way to learn, and a child that is "rescued from their crop" is done a great disservice. One grows by experiencing the fruit of decisions and behavior choices they have made. Dane's teacher has since apologized to him because she, because of a grudge (the fruit brought on by his behavior), had not given him the correct grade.

Darin played soccer through his senior year along with volleyball and tennis, which he enjoyed. After he graduated, he worked for a while then entered the Tech, taking liberal arts. He got a job with a telecommunications company, but after about a year or even less said, "Mom, I'm going to *have* to move to North Carolina. I miss Dane every day of my life!" He did and lived with friends in the house right across from Dane and Neva's, which Donny and his family had been able to rent when they moved down. (Again, God's kind provision.)

When Donny's family was able to move into their completed home, the little house became a nice bachelor pad, and Darin was quite an influence on one of the boys accepting the Lord. He too traveled for a time with his brothers selling merchandize for dc Talk and Steven Curtis Chapman.

Darin formed his own band, and also developed a CD playing all the instruments; keyboard, drums, lead and bass guitar, and doing the vocals, using songs he had written for the project. During this time he played in the church worship band.

The Lord opened the door for him to travel with a sister group, the Beu Sisters. He played guitar to accompany them on stage and did an occasional solo. He also drove the camper, carried their suitcases, and was a big brother to them. The Beu Sisters were the opening act for the Kelly Clarkson/Clay Aiken tour. Because of this connection, Darin lived for a while in Florida with his own construction business, and is now in North Carolina. He is in real estate and also works in construction for his brother, Dane. He sincerely wants to do the will of the Lord, and we are grateful for that.

Our Dear Extras

The Lord has had His hand on the children that were with us, though most of them have gone through troubled times.

Eugene, sadly, chose some difficult paths. He does know the way, and though we've seen very little of him, we trust he will get established in the love of Christ.

Sam was valedictorian, and I believe (though I'm not sure), also class president. He then went right to the marines and served for four years. Upon discharge, he entered the state tech and majored in accounting. He was also the gym teacher at the Christian school at that time. He married, and has two lovely daughters, and they definitely want to walk in the Lord's path. Sadly, his marriage has ended.

Sally married and has two sons. Unfortunately the young man had a severe drinking problem, and the marriage ended. She has remarried to a very nice gentleman and walks with the Lord. She is a very nice, thoughtful young lady. Thankfully, her first husband has turned to Christ, and he and his wife and boys are very active in their church. God is good.

Shirley married, and has a sweet daughter and son. Sadly, this marriage has ended. Shirley walks with the Lord, and is also taking college courses majoring in criminal justice. She is a very determined, hard-working girl, and very sweet.

Susie had a son, then married, and had two other boys. That marriage was very difficult and she moved to another area. She met a very nice young man, who became part of their lives. Sadly, Susie passed away suddenly, but we feel she was ready to meet our kind Savior. The young man has kept care of the boys, and walks with the Lord. We all really appreciate him and trust the Lord to bless him for his care.

I want to mention also that Sam, Sally, Shirley, and Susie have a brother whom I will call Sydney, who is married and has two sons. We love and pray for them, too.

Helen married and has two fine boys. That marriage, sadly, ended, but she has remarried to a very fine gentleman. She is a sweet girl, and walks with the Lord. She has been working as a secretary in a local large industry.

Henry has married, and has a darling son. He graduated from college, and for quite a while was the president of a small local bank. He then went into business with his father. He is very precious, and walks with the Lord.

As you may be able to tell, all these children, too, are very dear to us. They have told us at various times what being in our care has meant to them, and we are deeply grateful to have been given the privilege of having them with us. It truly brings us joy.

27

No Greater Joy

In 3 John 1:4 it says, "I have no greater joy than to hear that my children walk in truth." How true that is! The reason for the detail of the children's lives is to show clearly that God is well able to "turn things around." Things have not been easy, nor is everything perfect now. Until Jesus returns (and it may not be too long!) nothing will be perfect. But God in His kindness has truly been *kind*—beyond all we could ask or think. To Him be all the glory!

One thing I want to mention. All of our married children have nice homes. God absolutely cannot be bribed or bought—but He does see and is so very, very kind.

When we were at the "little house," World Vision was attempting to build little houses for Vietnamese families. The cost was fifty dollars. We put a jar on the table, and everyone put in all they could. In time, we were able to accumulate the fifty dollars and were therefore able to "build" a little house for a needy family. Could that have been a factor in the Lord's kindness toward us? Could it be because they all accepted the "extras" into the family without complaint? I don't know—but He is so kind. (See Hebrews 6:10).

One thing I know for sure is that we never, ever have to be afraid to give—our money, all that we have, and our very being. His love is so amazing!

Our Most Recent Blessing

At a wonderful outdoor party our children gave us for our fiftieth anniversary, I adapted the lyrics to an old song and added them to the bridge the Lord gave me. The verses, each dedicated to a different part of our family, were all sung to the tune of "I May Be Wrong (but I Think You're Wonderful)." Bob Merton, a member of the band Brother Dietze and the Dixie Boys who played the keyboard, figured out the melody through only five phone calls and accompanied me. It was a surprise to the family, and they seemed to enjoy it.

Chorus

I may be wrong, but I think you're wonderful!
I may be wrong, but I think you're grand!
I like your style, say,
I think it's marvelous!
I'm always wrong, but I think you're grand!

For Don

We were in school when I met you,
A track star and yet you were sweet.
Your musical talents amazed me,
Swept me right off of my feet.
You're always kind, say!
I think you're wonderful.
I'm glad you're mine and,
I think you're grand!

For Our Children

You came from the Lord and we praise Him!
You've filled our hearts with such joy!
You made our life so exciting
From the very first boy!
You came from God, say!
We think you're wonderful!
Mom's always right and
We think you're grand!

For Their Spouses

You were sent by the Lord, and we thank Him.
You're in our family by choice.
You gave us beautiful grandkids,
How we love every sweet voice.
You're sent by God, say!
We think you're wonderful.
Lord bless your life and
Give you His Hand.

To the Grandchildren

You're a gift from the Lord; we're so grateful!
We've loved you right from the start!
Christ loves you more so surrender,
Please give Him all of your heart!
Christ loves you so, say!
His way is wonderful!
His Word is truth and
Will guide your life.

For Our Friends

You are our friends and we love you.
You've been there for us through the years.
You joined us in funny adventures

And helped us in laughter and tears.
You are our friends, say!
We think you're wonderful!
Lord bless your lives and
Be close to you.

Closing

Dear ones, there is a line in a song that asks, "Who am I that the King would bleed and die for me? Who am I that He would say, 'Not My will but Thine'?" Honestly, when I look back on things that have happened in our lives, that is my heart. Who am I, and who are we, that the Lord should have been so very kind and merciful to us? We certainly are nothing special!

But like I said at the beginning, this book was written to especially encourage young mothers and fathers. Though the way may be hard, the Lord *loves* you! He has given you such a beautiful privilege—"little people" for you to love, guide, and teach to know Him. He *will* be your "ever-present help!" With His help and mercy you, too, will look back with hearts full of deep, deep gratitude and much, much, joy.

May He make this so real to you. I trust this writing has been an encouragement, given a little help, and even a smile or a chuckle. Lord bless you! Hugs!

To contact the author: wwwgrandkidsgalore@gmail.com